The Perpendicular height of the source of Tiber Creek above the level of the Tide in the said Creek

The Perpendicular height of the West branch above the tide in Tiber Creek

The Perpendicular height of the ground where the Capitol is to stand is above the tide of Tiber creek

The water of Tiber Creek may be conveyed on the high ground where the Capitol stands and after watering that part of the City may be destined to other useful purposes

Reedy Branch and that of the Tiber may be conveyed to the Presidents House

LAT. of CAPITOL 38 53 N.

Tiber Creek

CAPITOL

EASTERN BRANCH

PART OF MARYLAND WITHIN THE TERRITORY OF COLUMBIA

W9-AJN-975

SCALE OF POLES

100   200   300   400   500   600 Poles
1   2   3   4   5   6 Inches

The Entrance Hall seen from the North Portico, with emblems of office at the door of the Blue Room:

THE WHITE HOUSE
AN HISTORIC GUIDE

WHITE HOUSE
HISTORICAL
ASSOCIATION
*with the
cooperation
of the
National
Geographic
Society
Washington, D. C.*

the President's seal, the President's flag, and the flag of the United States.

THE WHITE HOUSE: AN HISTORIC GUIDE
TEXT CONSULTANTS: *Margaret B. Klapthor*, CURATOR, DIVISION OF POLITICAL HISTORY, SMITHSONIAN INSTITUTION; *Charles F. Montgomery*, CURATOR, THE MABEL BRADY GARVAN COLLECTION AND RELATED COLLECTIONS, YALE UNIVERSITY; *Dr. Richard L. Watson, Jr.*, PROFESSOR OF HISTORY, DUKE UNIVERSITY

CONSULTING EDITOR: *Franc Shor*, ASSOCIATE EDITOR, NATIONAL GEOGRAPHIC MAGAZINE
NATIONAL GEOGRAPHIC STAFF: *Robert L. Breeden*, EDITOR; *Donald J. Crump*, ASSOCIATE EDITOR AND PICTURE EDITOR; *Philip B. Silcott*, SENIOR ASSISTANT EDITOR; *William R. Gray*, MANUSCRIPT EDITOR; *Ann C. Resh and Jan N. Clarkson, Margery G. Dunn, Toni Eugene, Johanna G. Farren, Jane McCauley, Cynthia Russ Ramsay*, RESEARCH; *Geraldine Linder*, ASSOCIATE PICTURE EDITOR; *Peggy D. Winston*, STYLE; *Joseph A. Taney*, STAFF ART DIRECTOR; *Josephine B. Bolt*, ART DIRECTOR; *Ursula Perrin*, DESIGN ASSISTANT; *Robert W. Messer*, PRODUCTION; *Margaret Murin Skekel, Raja D. Murshed*, PRODUCTION ASSISTANTS; *John R. Metcalfe*, ENGRAVING AND PRINTING; *Joseph H. Bailey, James P. Blair, Victor R. Boswell, Jr., David R. Bridge, Nelson Brown, John E. Fletcher, Otis Imboden, Larry Kinney, Bates W. Littlehales, George F. Mobley, Albert Moldvay, Robert S. Oakes, Winfield Parks, Martin Rogers, Joseph J. Scherschel, Volkmar Wentzel*, PHOTOGRAPHY; *Jane H. Buxton, Virginia L. Grigsby, Suzanne J. Jacobson, Joan Perry*, STAFF ASSISTANTS; *Dorothy C. Corson, Toni Warner*, INDEX

White House staff members who assisted during the book's preparation: *Clement E. Conger*, WHITE HOUSE CURATOR; *Rex Scouten*, CHIEF USHER; *Betty Monkman and Carol Heinsius*, RESEARCH

"Flag Day," painted in 1917, is one of Childe Hassam's many studies on this theme. The painting, an impressionistic rendering of Fifth Avenue in New York City during a shower, hangs in the East Wing Lobby.

FOREWORD

Home of Presidents, the White House symbolizes to many the heart of American democracy, the focal point of our government. From its private offices come important decisions and policies that affect millions of people throughout the world. To its stately public rooms come throngs of American and foreign visitors eager to tour a living monument of the United States.

Mrs. John F. Kennedy's belief that the most famous American home, the White House, and its priceless furnishings should be preserved as an essential landmark in American history led to the formation of the nonprofit White House Historical Association. Its efforts have been warmly supported by succeeding Chief Executives and their First Ladies — by President and Mrs. Lyndon B. Johnson, and now by President and Mrs. Richard M. Nixon.

One of the initial purposes of the Historical Association was to publish an informative guidebook and make it readily available to the public. All net profits from the sale of the guidebooks are used to acquire furnishings and works of art associated with past Presidents of the United States, and for restoration projects in the White House. Such projects have included the renovation of the East Garden and the restoration of several rooms. The Historical Association also commissions the official portraits of each new President and First Lady.

Without private donations many of the improvements and acquisitions for the White House would be impossible. Gifts have varied from paintings and drawings worth thousands of dollars to a piece of velvet of exactly the right period, color, and design to cover a pair of chairs that Abraham Lincoln used.

Other donations come in different forms: The directors of the White House Historical Association are grateful to all those who have contributed to the publication of this guidebook. They are particularly indebted to the National Geographic Society — to Dr. Melvin M. Payne, President, and to Dr. Melville Bell Grosvenor, Editor-in-Chief. The Society, as a public service, has provided the photographs and text for the guidebook and has supervised its publication.

President and Mrs. Nixon hope that as many Americans as possible will visit the White House and profit from a sense of its history and traditions — both uniquely American. With equal pleasure they welcome visitors from other lands. They hope that all who tour the White House will depart with a feeling of our nation's rich heritage and stirring past.

David E. Finley

THE WHITE HOUSE

Our family is delighted
to welcome you to the
White House.

One of our greatest
pleasures is in sharing
with visitors the history,
beauty and treasures of
this residence belonging
to all Americans and
the home of Presidential
families since 1800.

May your visit be a
happy experience and one
which you will enjoy
reliving through the pages
of this book.

With best wishes,

Patricia Nixon

CONTENTS

I

A GUIDE TO THE MANSION

More than one and a half million visitors go through the White House every year, making it one of the most frequently toured homes in this country. The only residence of a head of state open to the public on a regular basis free of charge, the White House is a museum of American history — with portraits of Presidents and First Ladies, works by some of America's finest artists, antique furniture in authentic settings, and memorabilia of historic importance. It is also the home and office of the President of the United States, where the pressing business of Government is being conducted even as tourists visit nearby, admiring the mansion's many treasures from the past.

A painting on pages 102-103 of this book indicates the route of the tour through the White House and the locations of the most important rooms. Each tour begins in the wood-paneled East Wing Lobby and continues along the Ground Floor Corridor, up the wide marble staircase, and through the elegant rooms of the State Floor. Portraits of recent Presidents hang in the North Entrance, through which visitors pass as they leave the White House.

The first part of this book, "A Guide to the Mansion," describes, with historical notes, rooms open to the public and many that are not —some of the private family rooms on the second floor and the Presidential offices in the West Wing. The second part, "The Changing White House," traces, in illustrations and in words, the history of the mansion from its inception on the drawing board of architect James Hoban in 1792 through its many renovations.

Curving walk and driveway — shaded in spring by flowering magnolia — lead to the covered entranceway of the East Wing of the White House. Public tours of the Executive Mansion begin in the East Wing Lobby.

THE EAST WING

Most visitors to the White House enter through the East Wing Lobby, built in 1942, where portraits of Presidents and First Ladies hang on either side of the wood-paneled hall. Presidents John Tyler, William H. Taft, and Woodrow Wilson are represented here, as well as Mrs. Tyler and Mrs. Harry S Truman. The portrait of President Tyler was painted in the White House and shows the Bulfinch dome of the Capitol in the background.

At the end of the hall and up a few steps is the Garden Room, from which a glass-enclosed colonnade leads to the Ground Floor of the White House. The style of furniture used when this area was redecorated in 1971 gives it the look of a garden room during the Regency period (1811-1820, when the Prince of Wales, later George IV, was regent for his father, George III). The Regency style, an English neoclassical style, includes elements of *chinoiserie* — European adaptation of Oriental motifs in furniture design. The Regency-style yellow lacquered chairs are carved to look like bamboo; the painted sofa was made in England about 1820; the lacquered tables are 19th-century Chinese. The softly colored Spanish rug, chosen to blend with the waxed brick floor, was woven in the Savonnerie manner. (This term refers to a type of handmade carpet, produced by a French tapestry establishment which once stood on the site of a *savonnerie,* or soap factory.)

The delicate furniture, streaming sunlight, and topiary *Ficus* trees help to bring the mood of the adjacent garden into the room. The Jacqueline Kennedy Garden, so named in 1965 by Mrs. Lyndon B. Johnson, contains a variety of flowering trees, shrubs, and flower beds and is used primarily by the First Lady as an informal reception area.

A diagram, seen on the right in the photograph, explains the visitor's route through the mansion and marks the entrance to the colonnade, which was built in 1902 and reflects the original pavilion design approved by Thomas Jefferson. Large windows of antique handmade glass give the visitor a rather kaleidoscopic view of the garden on his way to the East Foyer, where a changing exhibit shows state gifts from foreign governments.

On the walls of the foyer are a number of large portraits of former Chief Executives, including Millard Fillmore, Chester A. Arthur, Grover Cleveland, and Calvin Coolidge. The two marble busts displayed along the foyer wall were bought by President James Monroe in 1817 from the son of George Washington's secretary, Tobias Lear. They represent important figures in American history, Christopher Columbus and Amerigo Vespucci, the Italian navigator and explorer of the New World after whom the continents of North and South America were named.

Francisco Anelli's portrait of Julia Gardiner Tyler (right), which hangs in the East Wing Lobby, was painted in 1848, three years after she lived in the White House. Mrs. Tyler suggested a First Lady portrait collection to President Andrew Johnson and donated her own to begin the tradition.

Above: A bronze inkstand, gift of a descendant of its original owner, Thomas Jefferson, is one of many small objects of historic interest displayed in changing exhibits along the colonnade.

GROUND FLOOR CORRIDOR

Until 1902 the Ground Floor Corridor and the rooms opening off of it were used as a work area. When Abraham Lincoln arrived at the White House in 1861, an aide recalled, the basement had "the air of an old and unsuccessful hotel." Even in the cold weather it reminded you "of old country taverns, if not of something you have smelled in the edge of some swamp."

Checking structural conditions in 1902, the New York architectural firm of McKim, Mead & White found that James Hoban's "fine, groined arches ... had been cut into in all directions" to hold pipes. The furnace room jutted into the corridor; heat mains and a fresh-air duct hung from the ceiling. As a result of the 1902 renovation and extensive remodeling during the Truman Administration, Hoban's elegant vaulted ceiling was restored to its clean simplicity and the hall transformed by walls and floors of marble, antique furniture, paintings, sculpture, and other works of art.

Selected pieces of White House china are now displayed in a Baltimore Sheraton-style breakfront bookcase. Two sculptures with Western themes by Frederic Remington and Charles Russell flank the entrance from the East Foyer.

The custom of hanging portraits of First Ladies in this area dates from 1902 when Mrs. Theodore Roosevelt wrote to Charles McKim asking that "all the ladies of the White House, including myself," be relegated to "the downstairs corridor...." Traditionally, portraits of the two most recent First Ladies have been displayed on either side of the Diplomatic Reception Room entrance. On the left is Aaron Shikler's portrait of Jacqueline Kennedy Onassis and on the right, Claudia "Lady Bird" Johnson by Elizabeth Shoumatoff.

Under the portraits are two similar pier tables (originally designed to fit into a pier, or space between two openings), one labeled by the New York cabinetmaker Charles Honoré Lannuier and the other attributed to him. Flanking these are four lattice-back chairs attributed to the workshop of Samuel McIntire of Salem, Massachusetts. The vases on the marble-top tables were ordered from Paris by President Monroe in 1817. Bronze figures by Thomas Ball, of Henry Clay and Daniel Webster, are displayed beside the doorway. Directly across the hall are two bronze heads: British Prime Minister Winston Churchill by Jacob Epstein and President Dwight D. Eisenhower by Nison Tregor.

At the far end of the corridor are portraits of Edith Galt Wilson, Sarah Childress Polk, and Caroline Harrison. Mrs. Harrison, a talented amateur artist, designed the Harrison china which is now displayed in the China Room and in the Family Dining Room.

The Ground Floor Corridor sparkles with three Regency chandeliers and provides an elegant gallery for visitors on their way to the State Floor. The President's seal, embedded in the North Entrance floor in 1902, was moved to the wall above the Diplomatic Reception Room doorway during the Truman renovation of 1948-52.

The Sheraton-style breakfront bookcase, made in Baltimore in 1803, displays a selection of Presidential china. During the Administration of Theodore Roosevelt, the Ground Floor Corridor was lined with cabinets containing the White House china collection which was started by Caroline Harrison in 1889 and greatly expanded by Mrs. Roosevelt. It had grown so large by 1917 that Edith Galt Wilson had it placed in a special area known today as the China Room. On the top shelf, center, stand plates used by George Washington at Mount Vernon; the shelf below displays Lincoln china.

GROUND
FLOOR
CORRIDOR

Douglas Chandor's 1949 portrait of Eleanor Roosevelt conveys her many moods and activities. Mrs. Roosevelt, reluctant to pose, inscribed the canvas: "A trial made pleasant by the painter."

"Coming Through the Rye," a bronze sculpture by Frederic Remington that was cast in 1902, depicts four spirited cowboys reveling at full gallop. An Easterner, Remington lived and traveled in the West and left a vivid record of its rugged life in his paintings and sculpture.

Elizabeth Shoumatoff painted this portrait of Mrs. Lyndon B. Johnson in 1968 with Mrs. Johnson's favorite view from the White House, the Jefferson Memorial, in the background. Lady Bird Johnson carried on Mrs. Kennedy's efforts to acquire objects of historical and artistic importance. She is, however, best known for her special interest in restoring and preserving America's natural landmarks— from large national park areas to the Capital City's many small parks which she filled with trees and flowers.

New York artist Aaron Shikler painted this portrait of Mrs. John F. Kennedy in 1970, seven years after she lived in the White House. Jacqueline Kennedy Onassis' New York apartment forms the background for the painting. Mrs. Kennedy was particularly concerned with the authentic restoration of the White House to reflect the times and tastes of the families who have lived there. She established a Fine Arts Committee to acquire historically important furnishings and works of art, and suggested the creation of the White House Historical Association.

THE LIBRARY

The Library was completely redecorated in 1962 as a "painted" room typical of the early 1800's. The paneling, now a warm ivory color, dates from the Truman renovation of 1948-52 when the White House, declared structurally unsound, was stripped to a shell as an alternative to razing it. A new steel framework was built under the foundation and some of the old timbers were used to make paneling for various ground-floor rooms. Right: two portraits by Charles Bird King of Indian emissaries who visited the mansion in 1821—Eagle of Delight, of the Oto Tribe, who died, shortly after she returned home, from measles contracted during the visit, and Sharitarish, or "Wicked Chief," of the Pawnee tribe.

PRESENTED TO THE WHITE HOUSE COLLECTION, 1962

"Tubs, Buckets and a variety of Lumber" cluttered Room 17 of the basement in February 1801, according to the first official White House inventory. The room served mainly as a laundry area until Theodore Roosevelt's renovation of the Ground Floor in 1902, when it was designated a "Gentlemen's Ante-room." In 1937, it was remodeled as a library for books selected by the Library of Congress and for first editions presented to the President by American authors and publishers. This wide-ranging collection, still being augmented, serves as a working library for the President, his family, and his staff.

The Library is furnished in the style of the late Federal period (1800-1820) with most of the pieces attributed to Duncan Phyfe, the New York cabinetmaker. It is less formal than the rooms of the State Floor and is often used for small teas and receptions. The soft tones of the paneling are complemented by a green-and-gold Aubusson rug. The gilded wood chandelier with a painted red band was made about 1800 and belonged to the family of James Fenimore Cooper, author of *The Last of the Mohicans* and other classics.

An unusual Federal-period looking glass, acquired in 1971, hangs on the north wall between the windows. The top portion contains a rare example of *églomisé* painting—reverse painting on glass—of an American eagle bearing the motto from the Great Seal of the United States in its talons. The looking glass, made in New York in the early 19th century, has a gilded wood architectural frame. Below the looking glass is one of a pair of Phyfe caned settees. In front of the windows are two of six matching Phyfe "cross-bannister" chairs with caned seats covered by cushions. The other settee is against the south wall opposite the windows. The octagonal library table in the center of the room and the pair of chairs near it are also attributed to Phyfe.

The neoclassical mantel on the west wall, from a house in Salem, Massachusetts, is attributed to the workshop of Samuel McIntire, master craftsman of that town. To the right of the fireplace is a Massachusetts Sheraton-style armchair; to the left is a New York armchair matching the Phyfe side chairs near the table. Beside the armchairs are two similar sewing or work tables with a pair of English Sheffield Argand lamps, a gift of the Marquis de Lafayette to Gen. Henry Knox, Secretary of War in Washington's Cabinet. Such lamps, named after their Swiss inventor, Aimé Argand, were a major innovation; George Washington ordered some in 1790, noting that by report they "consume their own smoke . . . give more light, and are cheaper than candles." Another pair, made in Boston about 1840, stand on the Sheraton-style desk near the east door.

One of the many Athenaeum portraits of George Washington by Gilbert Stuart hangs over the mantel. Stuart painted three portraits of Washington from life, the Vaughan portrait (1795), now in the National Gallery of Art; the full-length Lansdowne portrait (1796), now owned by the Pennsylvania Academy of the Fine Arts in Philadelphia; and the Athenaeum portrait (1796), acquired in 1876 by the Boston Athenaeum.

The lighthouse clock, patented in 1822 by Simon Willard of Roxbury, Massachusetts, has a fragile glass dome with an alarm bell inside. The medallion on the mahogany base shows the Marquis de Lafayette. Below: an Argand lamp presented by Lafayette to General Knox, his friend and comrade-in-arms.

Gilbert Stuart kept the Athenaeum portrait throughout his life and made well over 50 copies of it for patriotic Americans. The portrait in the Library was painted for a Baltimore family and, like all the copies, varies slightly from the original. Stuart also made copies of the Lansdowne portrait, one of which hangs in the East Room.

To the right of the mantel is a Phyfe card table that displays an unusual lighthouse clock made by Simon Willard. Hanging in the corner of the room is a long wooden pole which ingeniously unfolds to form a narrow ladder, called a "machan" or "howdah ladder." These were originally used in India for mounting and dismounting elephants — "machan" derives from a Hindu word for scaffolding and a howdah is the covered seat or pavilion on an elephant's back. The ladders were copied in England and used as library steps; this one is a reproduction of an English 18th-century version.

Four portraits of American Indians by Charles Bird King flank the east door, and a fifth hangs over the entrance to the corridor. The paintings, given to the White House in 1962, are King's own copies from a set of eight portraits commissioned in 1821 for the American Indian archives, then located in Georgetown. The originals, which were in the Smithsonian Institution, were destroyed by fire in 1865. The Federal Government, fearing that westward expansion would be met by violent opposition from the powerful and militant tribes of the Great Plains, invited a number of Indian leaders to visit America's most important cities and forts and to meet their "Great Father," the President. Government officials hoped to overawe these Indians with an impressive show of military strength, luxurious gifts, and elaborate ceremony.

When the Indians arrived in Washington, merchants fitted them out in military finery for an audience with President James Monroe. They were formally received by the President in the Red Room on February 4, 1822. With the help of interpreters, he thanked them for coming, spoke of the white man's strength and the blessings of peace, and offered to send missionaries to instruct them in Christianity and agriculture. The chiefs, impressed but feeling ill-at-ease in their new clothes, gravely replied that they admired the things they had seen but preferred their own life of trapping beaver and hunting buffalo. Sharitarish, their leader, added: ". . . we have plenty of land, if you will keep your people off it."

Each speaker laid a gift at the President's feet: moccasins, feathered headdresses, buffalo robes, and peace pipes. Before the party moved to the Blue Room for cake and wine, Sharitarish expressed the hope that Monroe would order the presents kept "in some conspicuous part of your lodge, so that when we are gone . . . if our children should visit this place, as we do now, they may see and recognize with pleasure the deposits of their fathers, and reflect on the times that are past." The gifts were unfortunately lost long ago and efforts to avoid fighting were finally unsuccessful.

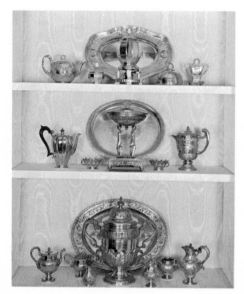

THE VERMEIL ROOM

Jean Honoré Fragonard's pencil-and-sepia drawing, "The Apotheosis of Franklin" (left), was one of the first gifts to the White House Fine Arts Committee in 1961. Vermeil pieces (far left) from the 18th, 19th, and 20th centuries include tea pots, cream and milk pitchers, platters, a covered chocolate pot (center of top shelf) and an English loving cup (center of bottom shelf).

The Vermeil Room, sometimes called the Gold Room, was completely refurbished in 1971 and serves as a display room and ladies' sitting room. The paneled walls have been painted a soft green to complement the collection of vermeil, or gilded silver, bequeathed to the White House in 1956 by Mrs. Margaret Thompson Biddle.

The Vermeil Collection, mostly French and English, dates from the Renaissance to the early 20th century and contains a variety of pieces from different services. The Biddle flatware, not on display, and some of the platters are often used on state occasions with the French gilt table service ordered by Monroe in 1817.

The green satin draperies are of early 19th-century design. The rug is a Turkish Hereke of about 1830, chosen for its pale-green background and gold silk highlights. The French neoclassical mantel, dating from about 1830 and installed in 1962, features two draped female figures in relief derived from caryatids, free-standing figures sometimes used as columns in Greek architecture.

To the left of the window is a Philadelphia classical pier table of exceptional quality made about 1815 with an inlaid-marble top. A posthumous portrait of Mrs. Andrew Jackson by Howard Chandler Christy hangs above it. The drum table in the middle of the room, a rare form in American furniture, was made in New York between 1810 and 1815 and is attributed to Duncan Phyfe. A pair of tables under the display niches in the west wall are in the American Empire style and are attributed to the New York workshop of Charles Honoré Lannuier. The gilt side chair to the right, made in England in the late 18th century, is one of six matching chairs in the room. The oil painting above the mantel, "Morning on the Seine," completed in 1897 by the French Impressionist Claude Monet, was given to the White House by the Kennedy family in 1963 in memory of President John F. Kennedy.

To the right of the doorway is a drawing by Jean-Honoré Fragonard, "The Apotheosis [or deification] of Franklin," executed in 1778 while Benjamin Franklin was in France to win support for the colonists' struggle against the British. This drawing, a classical allegory, depicts a laurel-crowned Franklin with his right hand invoking Athena to protect the seated figure of America and his left hand encouraging Mars to strike down Avarice and Tyranny in the foreground.

Also on the north wall is an 1804 portrait by Gilbert Stuart of Mrs. Richard Cutts, Dolley Madison's sister, to whom she wrote describing her flight from the White House when it was burned by the British in 1814. This portrait, acquired in 1972, is similar to the Stuart portrait of Dolley Madison in the Red Room.

THE CHINA ROOM

The "Presidential Collection Room," now the China Room, was designated by Mrs. Woodrow Wilson in 1917 to display the growing collection of White House china. The room was redecorated in 1970, retaining the traditional red color scheme determined by the portrait of Mrs. Calvin Coolidge—painted by Howard Chandler Christy in 1924. The day that President Coolidge was to pose for Christy, the Teapot Dome oil scandal broke, revealing serious Government corruption. The President was too preoccupied to sit for his portrait and Mrs. Coolidge posed instead. The

red theme continues in the velvet-lined cabinets, new silk taffeta draperies, and an English rug of about 1850, handwoven in the Savonnerie
manner. The cut-glass chandelier, made about 1800, is in the English
Regency style. The two American chairs flanking the mantel, called
"Martha Washington" or "lolling" chairs, were made in the early 19th
century. The painting "View on the Mississippi, Fifty-Seven Miles Below
St. Anthony Falls, Minneapolis" hangs above the mantel and was completed
by Ferdinand Richardt in 1858—the year Minnesota achieved statehood.

Every past President is represented in the China Room either by state china, family china, or glassware. The collection starts in the cabinets to the right of the fireplace and continues chronologically to the right.

Even the earliest Presidents received Government funds to purchase state china. However, by a special clause in the appropriation bills, "decayed furnishings" could be sold and the proceeds used to buy replacements. Such "furnishings" included state china and during the 19th century the cupboards were frequently swept clean and the contents carted off to auction. The money could then be used to order a new china service which better suited the President and his family. Much china, deemed unusable because of cracks or other damage, was given away. Large amounts were also lost through breakage. Thousands of dollars worth of china and glass were broken at the celebration following Andrew Jackson's inauguration, for example. Unruly crowds thronged the White House trying to catch a glimpse of the new President, who was finally forced to escape and spend the night at a boardinghouse.

Obviously, not much historical importance was attached to White House china during the first hundred years of the Presidency. In 1889, however, Mrs. Benjamin Harrison started to collect pieces from previous administrations, and her project was continued by Mrs. William McKinley. The collection was greatly expanded by Mrs. Theodore Roosevelt, who strongly opposed the sale of any White House china. She also stopped the practice of giving away or selling damaged china; it was broken and scattered into the Potomac River instead.

Many Presidents have chosen not to order new state china, either because it was not needed or because the appropriation was used for other things. Presidents usually take their family china with them when they leave the White House; most of the pieces in the collection have been acquired from their descendants or at auction.

Until the Administration of Woodrow Wilson all Presidential china was produced outside of the United States—usually in France or England—although some of the services were first designed by Americans. Patriotic symbols, especially the American eagle, have been frequently used in the china designs. The most recent state china to be ordered was Mrs. Lyndon B. Johnson's American wildflower service which was donated to the White House in 1968 and includes more than 200 place settings.

For unabashed assertion of national pride, no china could outshine the exuberant Hayes service; purchased in 1879, it portrays American flora and fauna. The game platter with a strutting wild turkey is one of a series of painted and sculpted plates decorated with wild animals, fish, fruits, and vegetables. When the china first appeared at a state dinner, according to one report, it formed "the most conspicuous part of the furniture of the table."

THE CHINA ROOM

Above: a serving platter from the flamboyant Hayes china, made in France by Haviland & Co. Early Presidential family china (bottom right): a Sèvres tureen owned by John and Abigail Adams; a Chinese export porcelain sugar bowl from Martha Washington's monogrammed personal china; a French cup and saucer, part of a service purchased by James Madison from James Monroe. Dolley Madison designed the monogram.

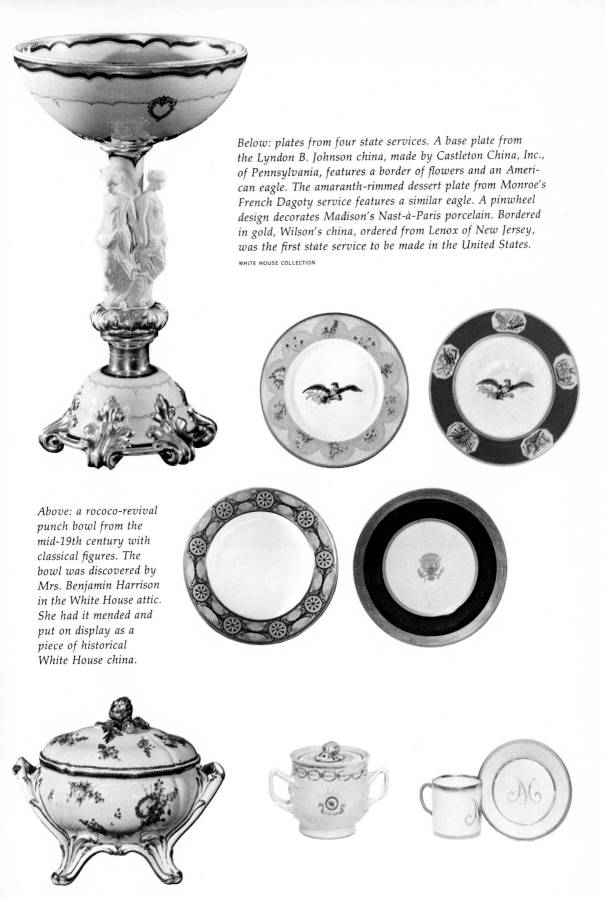

Below: plates from four state services. A base plate from the Lyndon B. Johnson china, made by Castleton China, Inc., of Pennsylvania, features a border of flowers and an American eagle. The amaranth-rimmed dessert plate from Monroe's French Dagoty service features a similar eagle. A pinwheel design decorates Madison's Nast-à-Paris porcelain. Bordered in gold, Wilson's china, ordered from Lenox of New Jersey, was the first state service to be made in the United States.

WHITE HOUSE COLLECTION

Above: a rococo-revival punch bowl from the mid-19th century with classical figures. The bowl was discovered by Mrs. Benjamin Harrison in the White House attic. She had it mended and put on display as a piece of historical White House china.

THE DIPLOMATIC RECEPTION ROOM

The Diplomatic Reception Room, once used as a boiler and furnace room, is now furnished as a drawing room of the early 19th century. It serves as a south entrance hall, a gathering room for the President and his guests at state functions, and occasionally as an informal reception area.

In 1960, during the Eisenhower Administration, the Diplomatic Reception Room was furnished in the styles of the Federal period (1788-1825) with many fine examples of the craftsmanship of New York and New England cabinetmakers. An oval rug was woven for the room in the Aubusson manner with the seals of the 50 states incorporated into the border. The present color scheme of gold and white was chosen at the same time to complement the rug.

Additional furniture was placed in the room in 1961 and the striking panoramic wallpaper added. The paper, called "Scenic America," was first printed in 1834 by Jean Zuber et Cie in Rixheim, Alsace. (Wallpaper was widely used in 19th-century America and covered many of the White House walls at that time.) The scenes, based on engravings of the 1820's, show American landscapes that were particularly admired by Europeans. Starting to the left of the doorway as you enter from the Ground Floor Corridor are the Natural Bridge of Virginia, Niagara Falls, New York Bay, West Point, and Boston Harbor. The wallpaper was printed with wood blocks on small sheets of paper which were then glued together into panels. The views are all somewhat fanciful; Boston Harbor is believed to be the most accurate. A later version of the Zuber wallpaper has been hung in the President's Dining Room. The landscape is the same, but the foreground scenes depict episodes from the American Revolution.

In 1971 a Regency chandelier was added and a new carpet woven to replace the original, which had become worn. The sofa, Pembroke table, and the armchair on the right are in the Hepplewhite style. The sweeping curved back and graceful reverse-curve arm supports of the sofa are typical Hepplewhite designs. The card tables flanking the sofa and the other armchair are in the Sheraton style.

Near the doorway to the South Grounds are a pair of settees and two matching chairs attributed to the New York workshop of Slover and Taylor. A New York Sheraton-style settee attributed to Duncan Phyfe stands in front of the fireplace.

One of the three oval rooms in the White House proper, the Diplomatic Reception Room exhibits American Federal-period furniture. On state occasions the room provides a handsome entrance from the South Grounds.

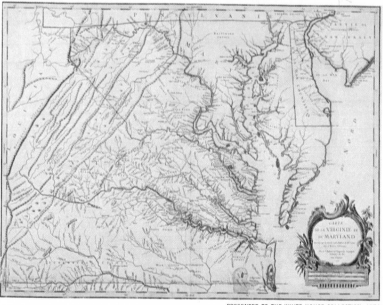

PRESENTED TO THE WHITE HOUSE COLLECTION, 1970

THE MAP ROOM

The Map Room, used by President Franklin D. Roosevelt as a situation room to follow the course of World War II, was redecorated in 1970 as a reception room in the Chippendale style, which flourished in America during the last half of the 18th century. Named after the English furniture designer Thomas Chippendale, this style combines the graceful lines of Queen Anne furniture with more elaborate rococo, Gothic, and Chinese carved motifs.

Cabinetmakers in Massachusetts and Rhode Island adapted the Chippendale style to a unique American furniture treatment termed "blockfront," in which the central of three vertical panels of a piece of furniture is recessed. A blockfront chest, made in Massachusetts about 1760, stands to the left of the window; to the right is a blockfront slant-top desk produced between 1760 and 1765 and bearing the carved-shell motif characteristic of the Townsends and Goddards, allied families of cabinetmakers from Newport, Rhode Island.

Notable among the American Chippendale pieces in the Map Room are an elaborately carved Philadelphia highboy against the wall opposite the windows, a Philadelphia rococo card table with rare hairy-paw feet situated under the antique map and attributed to Benjamin Randolph, a Philadelphia library table in front of the blockfront chest, and four chairs along the wall attributed to James Gillingham of Philadelphia—one carrying his label. A small mahogany lap desk for traveling, bearing the initials of its owner, Thomas Jefferson, stands on a Philadelphia Chippendale chest to the right of the mantel.

Above the blockfront desk is a portrait of Benjamin Franklin, completed in 1759 in London by Benjamin Wilson. It was removed from Franklin's house in Philadelphia during the American Revolution by a British officer, John André. André was later hanged as a spy by the Americans for his role as intermediary in Gen. Benedict Arnold's plot to betray West Point to the British in 1780. Gen. Charles Grey (later the first Earl Grey), once André's commanding officer, took the painting back to England. In 1906 the fourth Earl Grey returned the portrait in honor of the bicentennial of Franklin's birth.

The Map Room contains a number of 19th-century landscape paintings in the style of the Hudson River School. "Delaware Water Gap," painted by George Inness in 1861, hangs above the mantel. Also in the room is "Crossing the River Platte," painted in the late 1860's by Worthington Whittredge.

The rug, a brilliantly colored Heriz, is similar to other Oriental rugs used during the 19th century. The cut-glass chandelier, made in England about 1765, has rare star pendants.

Brightly colored rug and Chippendale-style furniture decorate the Map Room. Left: Rare 1755 French version of a map by colonial surveyors Joshua Fry and Peter Jefferson (Thomas Jefferson's father) hangs on the east wall, covering a case of current maps presented by the National Geographic Society.

THE
NORTH
ENTRANCE

The large North Entrance Hall and the Cross Hall formed part of James Hoban's original plans for the White House. The basic design has not been altered, although modifications have been made during various renovations. During the 19th century two principal stairways led to the second floor, the Grand Staircase being at the west end of the Cross Hall. In 1902 it was removed to increase the size of the State Dining Room; the remaining stairway, opening into the Cross Hall, was enlarged. During the 1948-52 renovation, this stairway was repositioned to open into the Entrance Hall.

The Cross Hall, with marble walls and floors added during the Truman renovation, is lighted by two Adam-style cut-glass chandeliers, made in London about 1790. The decorative plaster ceiling insets and the bronze light standards date from the Theodore Roosevelt renovation of 1902. A settee once owned by President Monroe stands beneath the 1960 portrait of Mrs. Dwight D. Eisenhower by Thomas E. Stephens.

At the east end of the Cross Hall hangs a portrait of President Eisenhower; a portrait of President Truman painted in 1947 by Greta Kempton hangs at the west end. Gilbert Stuart's 1801 portrait of Commodore John Barry and Francis Alexander's 1835 portrait of President Van Buren hang at the east end opposite Eisenhower's portrait. Two marble busts are displayed in niches along the south wall: Joel Barlow by Jean-Antoine Houdon and George Washington after Houdon.

The Cross Hall has not always had this look of elegant simplicity. In 1865 an inventory dismissed its furnishings as "all pretty common." Perhaps its most spectacular alteration occurred in 1882 when President Arthur called on Louis C. Tiffany of New York to redecorate the mansion. A stained-glass screen, reaching from floor to ceiling, was placed between the columns to divide the Cross Hall from the Entrance Hall. One observer remarked: "The light coming through the partition of wrinkled stained glass mosaic makes a marvelously rich and gorgeous effect, falling upon the gilded niches where stand dwarf palmetto trees, the silvery network of the ceiling, and the sumptuous furniture...." In these lavish surroundings the Grover Clevelands held their last dinner for the Diplomatic Corps, by then far too large for the State Dining Room. The McKinleys also gave dinners here. Apparently, the Tiffany screen did not block the flow of cold air from the North Entrance very effectively: "A gale roared through the improvised banquet hall whenever the front door was opened," writes historian Margaret Leech, "and the floor was so cold that the divans were robbed of cushions to make footstools for the ladies."

Until 1902, when the President's second-floor offices were moved to

The Cross Hall, leading from the State Dining Room to the East Room, is separated from the North Entrance Hall by Hoban's original colonnade. The state reception rooms open onto the right, or south, side of the Cross Hall. A life portrait of Dwight D. Eisenhower (right), painted by J. Anthony Wills in 1967, hangs in the Cross Hall near the East Room. A marble bust of American diplomat and poet Joel Barlow is displayed in a niche beyond the flags. It was executed in 1804 by the French sculptor Jean-Antoine Houdon.

PRESENTED TO THE WHITE HOUSE COLLECTION, 1967

PRESENTED TO THE WHITE HOUSE COLLECTION, 1963

Presidential portraits, a cut-glass chandelier, and red carpet on marble steps decorate the main stairway — the elegant passage between the Family and State Floors. In the Entrance Hall hang portraits of Lyndon B. Johnson (above), painted by Elizabeth Shoumatoff in 1968, and John F. Kennedy, painted by Aaron Shikler in 1970.

THE NORTH ENTRANCE

the newly built West Wing, the Entrance Hall served as a reception area and as a busy passageway. The furnishings were, by necessity, utilitarian and, judging from the inventories, consistently worn.

Today, the Entrance Hall, seen by visitors as they leave the White House, is decorated in the same style as the Cross Hall. Its furnishings include a French pier table purchased by Monroe in 1817 and a pair of French settees believed to have belonged to the Empress Josephine. A suite of early 19th-century gilded furniture in the French Empire style used by President Monroe was added to the Cross Hall in 1973. Portraits of John F. Kennedy and Lyndon B. Johnson hang on the west and east walls. By tradition, portraits of recent Presidents hang in the Entrance and Cross Halls.

The main stairway is often used on ceremonial occasions. Before state dinners, the President greets his guests of honor in the Yellow Oval Room and then they descend the stairs to the East Room where the other guests are gathered. Hanging along the stairway are portraits of 20th-century Presidents, including Franklin D. Roosevelt by Frank O. Salisbury, Woodrow Wilson by F. Graham Cootes, Warren G. Harding by F. Luis Mora, and William McKinley by Mrs. William Murphy; a portrait of Mrs. William Howard Taft by Bror Kronstrand is also in the stairway. Above the American pier table on the stair landing is a portrait of Herbert Hoover by Elmer W. Greene.

THE EAST ROOM

The East Room, scene of many historic White House events, was designated by Hoban as the "Public Audience Room." It normally contains little furniture and traditionally is used for large gatherings of many different kinds, including dances, after-dinner entertainments, concerts, weddings, funerals, church services, press conferences, and bill-signing ceremonies.

Today the East Room retains the early 19th-century classical style to which it was restored by architects McKim, Mead & White during the Roosevelt renovation of 1902. An oak floor of Fontainebleau parquetry was installed at that time as were the bronze electric-light standards, upholstered benches, and three Bohemian cut-glass chandeliers. The walls were paneled in wood with classical fluted pilasters and eight relief insets illustrating Aesop's fables. The paneling was painted white and delicate plaster decoration was added to the ceiling.

New marble mantels were installed over the four fireplaces during the Truman renovation of 1948-52. (The room was originally designed with two fireplaces in the west wall and five windows in the east wall. Latrobe's 1807 plan to wall in four of the five windows was adopted sometime during the early 19th century, and two new fireplaces were added.) In the early 1960's the mantels were painted off-white to match the walls and in 1965 gold damask draperies from France were hung at the windows. The gold-and-white color scheme was chosen by Mrs. Theodore Roosevelt although Charles McKim originally had envisioned crimson draperies. Red draperies were later substituted during the Franklin D. Roosevelt Administration but the Truman renovation returned the East Room to the gold-and-white theme. The Steinway grand piano with gilt American eagle supports was given to the White House in 1938.

The full-length portrait of George Washington which hangs in the East Room is one of several copies that Gilbert Stuart made of his original "Lansdowne" portrait of 1796 commissioned by Senator William Bingham. It is the only object known to have remained in the White House since 1800 — except for a period after the British burned the mansion during the War of 1812. Then Dolley Madison had refused to abandon the portrait as she fled; she wrote to her sister on the day of the fire: "Our kind friend, Mr. Carroll, has come to hasten my departure, and is in a very bad humor with me because I insist on waiting

The East Room, largest and most formal of the state reception rooms, remained unfinished until 1829. The present classical decor dates largely from the 1902 renovation; Martha Washington's portrait hangs on the east wall.

until the large picture of Gen. Washington is secured, and it requires to be unscrewed from the wall. This process was found too tedious for these perilous moments; I have ordered the frame to be broken, and the canvas taken out; it is done,—and the precious portrait placed in the hands of two gentlemen of New York, for safe keeping. And now, dear sister, I must leave this house, or the retreating army will make me a prisoner in it, by filling up the road I am directed to take. . . ." Her efforts were successful and the portrait was returned to the White House when the rebuilding was completed. The companion portrait of Martha Washington was painted by E. F. Andrews in 1878.

Although intended by Hoban to be the most elegant of the state reception rooms, the East Room remained unfinished for 29 years. It was here that the John Adams family, first occupants of the White House, dried their laundry, presumably with the help of two "Ten Plate" stoves listed in an inventory of February 26, 1801.

Thomas Jefferson partitioned the space to create two rooms for his secretary, Meriwether Lewis—later co-leader of the Lewis and Clark expedition—who had to move his quarters when the East Room ceiling fell in. Architect Benjamin Latrobe, appointed by Jefferson as Surveyor of Public Buildings, noted on a floor plan executed in 1803: "Public Audience Chamber—entirely unfinished, the cieling has given way." Jefferson's inventory of 1809 lists "34 armed Chairs black and Gold" in the "Large Unfinished Room," and "1 Table & Kettles for washing Tumblers," indicating that the room may have been used as a make-shift butler's pantry as well as a storage area. James Madison met with his Cabinet in the south end of the East Room, but whatever furnishings the room might have contained were destroyed in the fire of 1814 and no record of them remains.

After the fire, restoration of the White House included work on the "principal drawing room" and by November 21, 1818, Hoban reported that the floor had been laid, the walls and ceiling plastered, and the cornice, frieze, architrave, and decorative woodwork nearly finished. The appropriations, however, were not adequate to furnish the East Room properly. Four sofas and two dozen chairs were placed in the room but their upholstery was unfinished.

Four matching candelabra, purchased by President Monroe for the Blue Room in 1817, are displayed on the mantels of the west wall. Made of gilded bronze, they are thought to be the work of Pierre-Philippe Thomire, a French bronze caster.

President John Quincy Adams opened the room to provide space for the large New Year's Day receptions during his term; the furniture remained unupholstered. It was not until 1829 that Andrew Jackson finally decorated the room in grand style, at a cost to the taxpayer of over $9,000.

Jackson's purchases included "three 18-light" chandeliers with cut glass of "remarkable brilliancy," a "3-light centre lamp supported by female figures," eight "5-light" gilded wall brackets, and various table lamps. Four fireplaces were fitted with black-marble mantels with "Italian black and gold fronts"; four huge gilt-frame mirrors were placed above these mantels. Almost 500 yards of red-bordered Brussels carpet was purchased for the floor and lemon-yellow paper covered the walls. A clergyman from New England found this "great levee apartment . . . truly magnificent," carefully noting the "light-blue satin-silk" on the sofas and chairs and the "white, blue, and light-yellow commingled" hues of the curtains. Even if the ladies of his party agreed that the rich carpet "needed the cleansing effect of tea-leaves," he concluded that: "On the whole it is a seat worthy of the people's idol."

During the Civil War years and the Administration of Abraham Lincoln there was much activity in the East Room. At one time during the war Union troops occupied the room. In 1864 the East Room was the scene of a large reception given by President Lincoln in honor of Ulysses S. Grant shortly before his appointment as head of all the Union armies. In April of 1865 the East Room was again filled with people but this time they were mourners surrounding the body of President Lincoln as he lay in state on a black-draped catafalque. He had been assassinated by John Wilkes Booth, much as he had foreseen in a dream a few weeks earlier. Seven Presidents have lain in state in the East Room, including John F. Kennedy in November 1963.

Gilbert Stuart's 1796 portrait of George Washington was rescued by Dolley Madison shortly before the British burned the White House on August 24, 1814. The painting has been the property of the mansion since 1800.

Furnishings in the East Room had become shabby and worn by the time General Grant became President. In 1873 a drastic renovation transformed the East Room into a salon decorated in the Victorian style. The ceiling was divided into three sections with ornate false beams supported by gilded columns. Large gas chandeliers, patterned carpeting and wall coverings, heavy mirrors, and rich fabrics created what sometimes has been referred to as "steamboat palace" decor. In this setting President Grant's daughter, Nellie, was married in 1874 under a huge bell of roses. An elaborate wedding breakfast followed in the State Dining Room. (The next wedding to take place in the East Room was that of Alice Roosevelt and Congressman Nicholas Longworth in 1906. By that time, the room had been restored to the classic simplicity of the early 19th century.)

When President Arthur redecorated the White House in 1882, Louis C. Tiffany found it necessary only to install silver paper on the ceiling of the East Room and to increase the number of potted plants. All of these heavy Victorian adornments were swept away in the 1902 restoration. During the Theodore Roosevelt Administration, this room became the scene of some rather unusual activities, including a wrestling match arranged to entertain some 50 to 60 guests of the President. The exuberant Roosevelt children are also known to have used the East Room for roller skating.

THE
GREEN
ROOM

Although intended by Hoban to be the "Common Dining Room," the Green Room has served many purposes since the White House was first occupied in 1800. The inventory of February 1801 indicates that it was first used as a "Lodging Room." Thomas Jefferson, President after John Adams and the second occupant of the White House, used it as a dining room with a "canvass floor cloth, painted Green," foreshadowing the present color scheme. James Madison made it a sitting room since his Cabinet met in the East Room next door, and the Monroes used it as the "Card Room" with two card tables for the whist players among their guests. When the Monroes, the first occupants of the White House after the fire of 1814, set about refurnishing the mansion, they decorated the room with green silks. With the next President, John Quincy Adams, came the name "Green Drawing Room" and a green drawing room it has remained, traditionally serving as a parlor for small teas and receptions.

Not every President has chosen a green which everyone liked. The shade that Andrew Jackson approved provoked unfavorable comment from the ladies; they found the color "odious . . . from the sallow look it imparts." Styles in the room changed as frequently as the tastes of the Presidents until the time of Theodore Roosevelt, when it was furnished in the neoclassical style of early 19th-century America. However it was not until the Coolidge Administration that original pieces of Federal-period furniture were placed in the room.

The Green Room was completely refurbished in 1971. Its walls were re-covered with the delicate green watered-silk fabric originally chosen by Mrs. Kennedy in 1962. Draperies of striped beige, green, and coral satin—a major part of the 1971 renovation—were carefully designed from a document of the Federal period. The coral and gilt ornamental cornices are surmounted by a pair of handcarved, gilded American eagles with outspread wings. The eagle, patriotic symbol of the United States, was one of the favored decorative motifs of the Federal period and appears in many forms in this room.

The rug is a Turkish Hereke carpet of a 19th-century design with a multi-colored pattern on a green field. This green background, common in small Moslem prayer rugs, is unusual in a rug of this size.

The cut-glass chandelier, a gift to the White House during the Hoover Administration, was made in England about 1790. The plaster ceiling

The Green Room, a first-floor reception room, was completely refurbished in 1971. Its furniture is in the styles of the Federal period with many pieces attributed to Duncan Phyfe, a famous New York cabinetmaker.

As wife of the Secretary of State, Louisa Catherine Adams posed for Gilbert Stuart in 1821, four years before her husband, John Quincy Adams, became President. This is the first portrait of her to hang in the White House and is displayed in the Green Room (left). "Farm-yard in Winter" (below) is one of several paintings by George H. Durrie with that title. This scene, painted in 1858, depicts a Connecticut farm of about 1825. The unusual work table (right), one of two flanking the mantel, has a hinged lid which opens to reveal trays and small compartments. It may have been designed for fine sewing or possibly painting miniatures. The

Argand lamp, named after its Swiss inventor Aimé Argand, was ingeniously designed with a tubular wick to burn brighter and cleaner than other lamps of the late 18th century.

medallion above the chandelier, adapted from designs of the Federal period, was installed in 1971.

In "a noble, or genteel house," wrote Thomas Sheraton, the English furniture designer, a drawing room "should possess all the elegance embellishments can give." Most of the furnishings now in the Green Room date from 1800-1815, the period of Sheraton's greatest influence on American decor. Many of the pieces are attributed to the New York workshop of the well-known Scottish-born cabinetmaker, Duncan Phyfe, who enjoyed a reputation for fine design and excellence of craftsmanship.

Between the windows on the south wall is a secretary desk made in Baltimore about 1800 in the Hepplewhite style—named for George Hepplewhite, another English cabinetmaker whose book of furniture designs influenced style during the Federal period. A finial of a gilded American eagle with outstretched wings stands in the broken-arch pediment of the desk. A collection of early 19th-century Chinese export porcelain in the Green Fitzhugh pattern is displayed on the shelves and features a sepia-and-gold American eagle with the motto from the Great Seal: *E Pluribus Unum.* A New York armchair whose seat frame bears the signature of Lawrence Ackerman, one of Duncan Phyfe's upholsterers, stands before the desk. Above hangs "Still Life with Fruit," painted about 1862 by the American artist Rubens Peale. In the window niches are a pair of rare Duncan Phyfe benches made about 1810 for Robert R. Livingston. A distinguished New Yorker who helped to draft the Declaration of Independence, Livingston served as the first Secretary for Foreign Affairs from 1781 to 1783, and administered the oath of office to George Washington in 1789.

In front of the settee on the west wall is a New York sofa table with unusual clover-leaf drop ends. The two Sheraton mahogany armchairs near it, probably made in Philadelphia about 1810, are rare for the period because of the upholstered backs, indicating their intended use in a drawing room. (Typical Sheraton open-back chairs could also be used in a dining room.) On the sofa table are several historic pieces of White House silver, the most important being a Sheffield silver-plate coffee urn of about 1785 which belonged to John Adams. Given to the White House in 1964, it was considered by President Adams to be among his "most prized possessions." An engraved, ribbon-hung ellipse above the spigot bears the initials "JAA"—John and Abigail Adams. Flanking the urn are a pair of French candlesticks which were bought by Madison from Monroe in 1803 and appear in subsequent inventories of the Madisons' household furnishings.

The neoclassical marble mantel on the east wall is one of a pair ordered by Monroe from France and installed in the State Dining Room. During the Roosevelt renovation of 1902 this one was moved to the Green Room and the other to the Red Room. The *bronze-doré* clock with the seated figure of the Roman goddess Minerva, was one of two included in Monroe's purchases from France in 1817.

Above the mantel hangs a 1971 addition to the room—a New York convex girandole mirror with sconces, made about 1820. The gilded wooden frame has a large American eagle on the pediment and, significantly, a much smaller British lion below. On each side of the fireplace are two almost identical, small, and exceedingly rare mahogany work tables ingeniously designed with hidden compartments. They are attributed to the New York workshop of Charles Honoré Lannuier and were probably made about 1810. A pair of Sheffield Argand lamps with oval-back mirrors—made in England in the early 19th century—stands on the work tables.

Of particular note are two Sheraton chairs which flank the mantel, attributed to Duncan Phyfe's workshop and now upholstered in coral cut velvet. The one on the right is an armchair acquired in 1971 and signed "Stephen van Rensselaer—Albany—Stuffed by L. Ackerman, New York." The one on the left is a rare wing chair of about 1810.

Doors opening to the East Room are on either side of the mantel. Above the left door is a portrait by Daniel Huntington of Rutherford B. Hayes, the first President ever sworn into office in the White House. Above the right door is a portrait of President Benjamin Harrison by Eastman Johnson.

On the north wall, opposite the windows, are portraits by Gilbert Stuart of John Quincy Adams, painted in 1818, and his wife. The pair remained in the Adams family until a great-great-grandson, the present John Quincy Adams, presented them to the White House in 1970 and 1971. It is likely but not certain that the paintings hung in the White House during Adams's Presidency.

In 1816 Secretary of State James Monroe commissioned John Vanderlyn to paint a portrait of President James Madison (above left). When he succeeded Madison to the Presidency, Monroe was painted by Samuel F. B. Morse, best known as inventor of the telegraph but also a sucessful portrait artist. The likeness of Monroe (above) is assumed to be the one painted by Morse in the White House and completed in December 1819.

THE
GREEN
ROOM

"Niagara Falls," a Hudson River School painting of about 1835 by John Frederick Kensett, hangs above the door leading to the Cross Hall and complements the green motif of the walls. On the west wall of the Green Room (right), hangs the portrait of Benjamin Franklin by the Scottish artist David Martin. Painted in London from life in 1767, it shows a scholarly and aging Franklin with wig, spectacles, and ruffled shirt.

Below the portraits hang two newly acquired paintings of New England farm scenes: "Farmyard in Winter," on the right, painted in 1858 by George H. Durrie, and on the left, a fall scene entitled "Rainbow in the Berkshire Hills," completed in 1869 by George Inness of the Hudson River School.

A pair of mahogany pedestal pier tables of exceptional quality, made about 1817 in the workshop of Duncan Phyfe, stand below the landscapes. The clover-leaf tops are carved from grayish-green and white King of Prussia marble quarried near Philadelphia. Separated for many years, both tables were given to the White House in 1971.

On the west wall hangs the portrait of Benjamin Franklin by David Martin, the first major work acquired by Mrs. Kennedy's Special Committee on Paintings in 1962; it is considered by many art critics to be one of the finest portraits in the White House Collection. Below is an historically important American cityscape of the 19th century, "Philadelphia in 1858," by Ferdinand Richardt. The painting was found in India, restored, and given to the White House in 1963. On each side of this painting are matching mahogany and gilt mirrored wall sconces of about 1800. The superb design and quality of the carving suggest the hand of Samuel McIntire, a noted craftsman working in Salem, Massachusetts.

Below the paintings is a handsome Duncan Phyfe settee of about 1810 which bears distinctive trademarks of his design — the tied reeds and clustered wheatears carved on the crest rail, the outcurved arms, and the reeded legs and seat rail. Flanking the settee are a pair of "cluster-columned" drop-leaf library tables also attributed to Duncan Phyfe's workshop.

Two portraits hang on the west wall: President James Madison by the American artist John Vanderlyn and President James Monroe attributed to Samuel F. B. Morse.

THE
BLUE
ROOM

The oval Blue Room was completely redecorated in 1972 with many of the furnishings in the French Empire style—the decor chosen for the room by President James Monroe in 1817. Seven of the original gilded chairs fashioned for Monroe by Parisian cabinetmaker Pierre-Antoine Bellangé form the nucleus of the present furnishings. The Empire style originated in France during Napoleon's reign as Emperor and is characterized by richly carved rectilinear furniture based on Greek, Roman, and Egyptian forms. Typical decorative motifs that are evident in the Blue Room include acanthus foliage, imperial eagles, wreaths, urns, stars, and classical figures. Swags and brass mountings were commonly used in drapery designs.

The "elliptic saloon," with the oval rooms above and below it, formed the most elegant architectural feature of Hoban's plans for the White House. For the south wall of the Blue Room he designed French doors flanked by long windows. An oval portico with curving stairs was included in these original plans but was not built until 1824.

The Blue Room has always been used as a reception room except for a brief period during John Adams's Administration when it served as a south entrance hall. During the Madison Administration, architect Benjamin Latrobe designed a suite of classical-revival furniture for the room but only some working drawings remain; the furnishings were destroyed in the fire of 1814.

When President Monroe redecorated the "large oval room" after the fire, he used the French Empire style. Monroe ordered a suite of French mahogany furniture through the American firm Russell and La Farge, with offices in Le Havre, France. However, the firm shipped gilded furniture instead, asserting that "mahogany is not generally admitted in the furniture of a Saloon, even at private gentlemen's houses." The order included a pier table; two large *canapés*, or sofas; 18 armchairs; two *bergères*, or armchairs with enclosed and upholstered sides, for the President and First Lady; 18 side chairs; four upholstered stools; and six footstools. Monroe's purchases for the Blue Room also included two large looking glasses; two screens; a *bronze-doré* clock; curtains hung over arched gilt poles with eagles in the center; crimson flock wallpaper; various lighting devices; ornaments in glass, porcelain, and *bronze-doré*; and an oval Aubusson rug, woven especially for this room and described in the bill of sale as green velvet with the national arms in the center. The furniture was decorated with carved sprigs of olive, although Monroe had asked for eagles. The upholstery was listed as double-warp satin in delicate crimson and two shades of gold, with an American eagle woven into the center of a wreath of laurel, the classical symbol of victory.

The bill from Russell and La Farge described these and other articles as "for the Account and Risk" of the President. In fact, Monroe ran some political risk, since there was considerable public pressure to buy only those goods made in the United States. William Lee, who was in charge of ordering the furniture, wrote somewhat defensively: "It must be acknowledged that the [French] articles are of the very first quality. . . ." Lee praised Bellangé's suite as "substantial heavy furniture, which should always remain in its place, and form, as it were, a part of the house; such as could be handed down through a succession of Presidents, suited to the dignity and character of the nation."

In 1837, President Van Buren redecorated the oval salon and started the tradition of a "blue room." In 1860, however, President Buchanan sold the Bellangé chairs and sofas at auction and replaced them with a Victorian rococo-revival suite; it served into Theodore Roosevelt's Administration. Some of Monroe's other purchases were retained, including the Bellangé pier table, a French clock, and certain of the ornaments.

The Hannibal clock, displayed on the mantel, was the work of Denière and Matelin, noted French bronze casters who made many of the bronze-doré objects purchased in 1817.

WHITE HOUSE COLLECTION

In the renovation of 1902, McKim, Mead & White restored the Empire decor and designed a set of furniture for the Blue Room based on the Bellangé originals. The walls were covered with a heavy ribbed steel-blue silk, woven to match a sample from the Napoleonic era. The new oak floor of herringbone parquet was uncarpeted.

Blue fabrics served as both wall coverings and draperies during much of the 20th century, until 1962 when the room was redecorated and the walls covered with cream-colored striped satin. By that time, the White House had been given three of the original Bellangé chairs, from which additional copies were made. A fourth chair was acquired in 1963.

Thomas Jefferson as Vice President: an 1800 life portrait by Rembrandt Peale that was popularized by engravings.

In 1972 the room was again completely redecorated, other Empire furnishings were bought, and one of the original Bellangé *bergères* was returned to the White House as a gift. The fabric on the walls was replaced with wallpaper—an American silk-screen reproduction of a French Directoire paper made in 1800—with a blue frieze around the top and bottom derived from classical motifs. The new draperies, copied from an early 19th-century French document, are blue satin with handmade fringe and gold satin valances. The patterned blue silk upholstery is based on the original Monroe fabric, recorded in John Vanderlyn's portrait of James Monroe.

The early 19th-century French Empire gilt wood chandelier is encircled by acanthus leaves—an Empire motif also found in the wallpaper frieze, the new cornice, and the oval plaster ceiling medallion above the chandelier.

The French *torchères* in front of the windows, made about 1810 and given to the White House in 1962, are in the form of classical female figures holding candelabra. A pair of 19th-century Louis XVI gilded console tables with marble tops stands in the piers between the windows. To the left of the center window hangs an 1810 portrait of Andrew Jackson in uniform painted by John Wesley Jarvis. To the right is a portrait of Thomas Jefferson by Rembrandt Peale, painted in 1800 in Philadelphia when Jefferson was Vice President. Jefferson was pleased with the painting, from which two engravings were subsequently made.

Other noteworthy paintings in the Blue Room include a portrait of John Adams (on the west wall to the right of the windows) that was painted by John Trumbull in 1800 just before Adams became President. This is the first portrait of John Adams painted from life to be displayed in the White House and was added to the room in 1972. Also hanging on the west wall is an 1859 portrait of John Tyler by George P. A. Healy; it is considered to be the finest of the series of Presidential portraits Healy painted for the White House under a commission from Congress. Among the documents illustrated in the portrait is one pertaining to Texas, which was admitted to the Union in 1845, the last year of Tyler's Administration.

THE BLUE ROOM

One of Rembrandt Peale's many oval "porthole" portraits of George Washington hangs over the doorway to the Cross Hall. Flanking the doorway are two maritime scenes by Fitz Hugh Lane: "A View of Boston Harbor," painted in 1854, on the left, and "Baltimore Harbor," painted in 1850, on the right. To the right of the mantel is a portrait of Zachary Taylor in uniform wearing medals from the Mexican War. It was painted in the mid-19th century by an unknown artist. To the left of the mantel is a portrait of James Monroe from a set of five Presidential portraits painted by Gilbert Stuart between 1818 and 1820. The head was copied from a life portrait painted by Stuart in 1817.

The early 19th-century marble mantel on the east wall, acquired in 1972, is in the neoclassical style and is similar to the two mantels purchased by Monroe from France. Above it is a New York Federal looking glass surmounted by a spread-wing black American eagle. The precedent for such overmantel looking glasses in the Blue Room was set during the term of James Madison.

One of the two Empire clocks purchased by Monroe is displayed on the mantel. Called the Hannibal clock, it bears a standing figure of the famous general from Carthage who led his troops, with some 40 elephants, across the Alps to fight the Romans in 218 B.C. The French porcelain vases on the mantel, made in Sèvres about 1800, were originally purchased by Monroe for the "Card Room"—now the Green Room. The vases are decorated with painted scenes of Passy, the Paris suburb where Benjamin Franklin lived when he was Minister to France. The *bronze-doré* wall sconces hanging on either side of the looking glass were made in France about 1810. Winged creatures such as the griffins that support the candle arms were frequently used as decorative motifs on Empire furniture.

Under the Monroe portrait is one of a pair of fine English console tables made in the French manner between 1785 and 1790. The tables are most likely the work of a French craftsman living in England, which would explain the French influence in the details. Another pair of recently acquired console tables is displayed under the Fitz Hugh Lane paintings. The Louis XVI half-moon tables with marble tops are attributed to George Jacob, a French cabinetmaker of the late 18th century. Console tables were rarely signed as they were usually attached to the wall and considered part of the architecture of the room.

The Blue Room rug is a mid-19th-century dark-blue Savonnerie with an oval sunburst medallion in the center. The border design combines Empire motifs similar to those appearing in the wallpaper.

This Bellangé bergère— an armchair with closed and upholstered sides—was purchased in 1817 by James Monroe.

PRESENTED TO THE WHITE HOUSE COLLECTION, 1972

Above a white Carrara marble mantel in the Blue Room, a Federal looking glass reflects George P. A. Healy's portrait of President John Tyler. Grouped in front of the fireplace are Bellangé armchairs and Louis XVI occasional tables; Gilbert Stuart's portrait of James Monroe hangs to the left.

THE
RED
ROOM

Furnished in the Empire style of 1810 to 1830, the Red
Room—one of the four state reception rooms in the
White House—contains several pieces of furniture from
the New York workshop of the French-born cabinetmaker
Charles Honoré Lannuier. An 1842 portrait by Henry
Inman of Angelica Singleton Van Buren, President Martin
Van Buren's daughter-in-law and official hostess, hangs
above the mantel. A white marble bust of Van Buren in
the neoclassical style appears in the portrait; it is one
of three busts of Van Buren executed by Hiram Powers,
for whom the President posed in 1836. One of these
busts is displayed on the wall between the windows.

Benjamin Latrobe's 1803 drawing of the State Floor indicates that the Red Room served as "the President's Antichamber" for the Cabinet Room or President's Library next door. During the Madison Administration the antechamber became the "Yellow Drawing Room" and the scene of Dolley Madison's fashionable Wednesday night receptions. In "that centre of attraction," said a lady who knew her well, one saw "all these whom fashion, fame, beauty, wealth or talents, have render'd celebrated." Throughout the years, the room has served as a parlor or sitting room.

In 1972 the Red Room was redecorated, preserving the American Empire style chosen in 1962 during the John F. Kennedy Administration. The furniture displays many motifs similar to those of the French Empire pieces now in the Blue Room. The elegance of the Red Room furniture derives from a combination of richly carved and finished woods with *ormolu* mounts (decorative hardware made of gilded brass or bronze) in characteristic designs such as dolphins, acanthus leaves, lions' heads, and sphinxes. Egyptian motifs were extensively used in French Empire furnishings following Napoleon's 1798-99 campaign in Egypt, and many of these same designs were adopted by cabinet-makers working in New York, Boston, and Philadelphia.

The furniture in the Red Room dates from about 1810 to 1830. The rare mahogany secretary-bookcase between the windows is attributed to Charles Honoré Lannuier and exhibits the characteristic Empire rectilinear shape and ornamental brass hardware. The lancet arches in its glazed doors reflect a Gothic motif. The mahogany sofa table to the left of the fireplace, also attributed to Lannuier, has gilt winged caryatid supports and the paw feet commonly used in Empire furniture. Lannuier's labeled masterpiece, and the most important piece of American Empire furniture in the White House Collection, is the round marble-top *guéridon* opposite the fireplace. This table is made of mahogany and various fruitwoods with a *trompe-l'oeil* top of inlaid marble. *Bronze-doré* female heads surmount the delicately carved and fluted legs.

To the right of the fireplace is a graceful American Empire sofa with gilded dolphin feet. The sofa has the distinctive Empire curved back rail and scrolled arms. Behind it is a New York Empire card table, one of five tables in the room with a carved lyre design. An ancient stringed musical instrument, the lyre was widely used in Empire furniture as a decorative motif for table supports and chair backs.

The *bronze-doré* clock on the mantel, made by the well-known Parisian bronze caster Pierre Joseph Gouthière, was given to the White House by President Vincent Auriol of France in 1952. The clock was designed during the late 18th century to play pastoral music every hour on a miniature organ inside the gilded case.

The early 19th-century French gilt porcelain vases on either side of the clock are decorated with likenesses of George Washington and the Marquis de Lafayette. To the right of the fireplace is an American

Empire music stand holding sheet music for a march composed in honor of Lafayette's return to the United States in 1824.

During the 19th century the Red Room was often used as a music room and the furnishings occasionally included a piano or other musical instruments, such as the pianoforte and guitar ordered by Dolley Madison.

All the fabrics now in the Red Room were woven in the United States from French Empire designs. The walls are covered by a red twill satin fabric with a gold scroll design in the border. The furniture upholstery is a damask of the same shade of red. An early 19th-century design inspired the draperies made of gold satin with red damask valances and handmade gold-and-red fringe. The mid-19th-century English rug, woven in the Savonnerie manner, is beige, red, light blue, and gold; it was purchased for the room in 1971. The white marble mantel with caryatid figures is one of a pair ordered by Monroe and originally placed in the State Dining Room. The gilded French Empire chandelier was made about 1805.

Descriptions in contemporary accounts and bills of sale indicate that Monroe purchased furnishings for the Red Room, as well as the Blue Room, in the prevailing Empire style, which originated in France under Napoleon. This style suited Monroe's desire to furnish the house in a manner that he considered appropriate to the dignity of the nation.

The room was called the Washington Parlor during the Polk and Tyler Administrations, when it contained Gilbert Stuart's portrait of George Washington. President and Mrs. Lincoln used the Red Room frequently for informal entertaining, and a contemporary reporter noted that the furniture was "very rich — of crimson satin and gold damask, with heavy gilded cornices to the windows and a profusion of *ormolu* work, vases, etc., some of which is very ancient, being bought or presented during Monroe's and Madison's Administrations."

John Singer Sargent portrayed Theodore Roosevelt as a forceful man pausing to speak on a White House staircase. The President's impatience and reluctance to pose caused difficulties for the artist.

Photographs taken during the latter half of the 19th century indicate that Victorian furnishings had been introduced to the Red Room. During the Theodore Roosevelt renovation of 1902, many of these Victorian furnishings were removed from the room and the collection of First Lady portraits which had hung there toward the end of the 19th century was transferred to the Ground Floor Corridor at the request of Edith Kermit Carow Roosevelt.

Dolley Madison's portrait (above), painted by Gilbert Stuart in 1804, is believed to have hung in the Red Room in 1813 and was presumably rescued from the fire of 1814 along with Stuart's portrait of George Washington and the Madisons' books and silver. An Empire sofa of about 1825 behind the round marble-top guéridon is flanked by a pair of mahogany card tables acquired in 1971. On the wall hang two gilt wood eagle sconces made in England in the late 18th century. A still life by Severin Roesen, painted about 1850, hangs below Dolley Madison's portrait on the north wall. One of a pair of Boston lyre tables (above), made about 1815 and acquired in 1971, is displayed under the Roesen painting. The tables are made of rosewood with ormolu mounts. A French Empire 36-light chandelier, made in 1805, hangs in the center of the Red Room and is fashioned of carved and gilded wood. "The Last of the Mohicans," completed by Asher B. Durand in 1857, hangs above the sofa; a portrait of Col. William Drayton, painted by Samuel F. B. Morse in 1818, is above the Durand painting. Displayed on the sofa table is a marble bust of Henry Clay by sculptor Joel T. Hart.

THE STATE DINING ROOM

The State Dining Room, which now seats as many as 140 guests, was originally much smaller and served at various times as a drawing room, office, and Cabinet Room. Not until the Administration of Andrew Jackson was it called the "State Dining Room," although it had been used for formal dinners by previous Presidents.

As the nation grew larger, so did the invitation list to official functions at the White House. In 1856 a reporter remarked that the State Dining Room was "not large enough, being 30 feet by 25 . . . as the Executive entertains Congress, the Supreme Court, diplomats and most of the distinguished people who visit Washington at his table, he requires a commodious and convenient dining-room." Toward the end of the 19th century, large dinners had to be held in the Cross Hall or the East Room.

Such inconvenient makeshifts became unnecessary after the renovation of 1902 when architects McKim, Mead & White removed the main stairway from the west end of the Cross Hall and enlarged the State Dining Room to its present dimensions. The two Italian-marble mantels installed by Monroe were moved to the Red and Green Rooms and a single larger fireplace constructed in the west wall. The architecture of the room was modeled on that of neoclassical English houses of the late 18th century. Below a new ceiling and a cornice of white plaster, natural oak wall paneling with Corinthian pilasters and a delicately carved frieze was installed. Three gilded eagle console tables were placed against the walls, and a silver chandelier and silver wall sconces were also added.

The dining room, when furnished, strongly reflected President Theodore Roosevelt's enthusiasm for big-game hunting. At his request, buffalo heads were carved on the new stone mantel, a large moose head was hung above the fireplace, and other big-game trophies were placed on the walls. Two ornate 17th-century Flemish tapestries also decorated the wood paneling, and new draperies of rich green velvet were installed. An architectural historian hailed the new dining room as "a stately hall of the Early English Renaissance." A critic, in the *Architectural Record* of April 1903, approvingly wrote that a White House "all carried out in strict Colonial would be but a monotonous and insipid mansion."

The 1902 classical woodwork was preserved in the Truman renovation of 1948-52 and was painted for the first time—a soft celadon green. Roosevelt's big-game trophies had long since been removed from the dining room. (The heads were sent to the Smithsonian Institution in 1923. Mrs. Theodore Roosevelt retrieved five of them in 1934 and six

The mahogany dining table, surrounded by Queen Anne-style chairs, displays part of Monroe's gilt service purchased from France in 1817. The bronze-doré ornamental pieces are used today as table decorations for state dinners. The plateau centerpiece measures 13 feet 6 inches in length when fully extended into seven mirrored sections. Standing bacchantes holding crowns for candles or tiny bowls border the plateau. Three fruit baskets, supported by female figures, are filled with flowers. The two rococo-revival candelabra had been added to the collection by the late 19th century.

THE STATE DINING ROOM

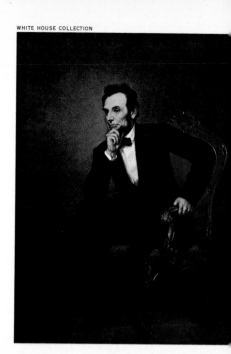

Gold damask draperies drawn for evening, the State Dining Room is prepared for a formal dinner of 111 guests. The china was ordered by the Lyndon B. Johnsons and the glassware by the John F. Kennedys. The plateau combines with other pieces of Monroe's gilt service and vermeil flatware from various administrations to complete the table setting. Above the mantel hangs George P. A. Healy's portrait of Abraham Lincoln, painted in 1869 and later acquired by the President's son, Robert Todd Lincoln. Robert's widow bequeathed the painting to the White House in 1939.

are still there.) During the Truman renovation the original marble mantel with buffalo heads was replaced by a simple, black marble mantel. A reproduction of the buffalo-head mantel was installed in the State Dining Room in 1961.

At that time the wood paneling was painted antique ivory and the sconces and chandelier were gilded. In 1967 the Queen Anne-style chairs—chosen for the room in 1902—were reupholstered with gold cut velvet of an Italian Renaissance floral design popular in the late 18th century, and new silk-damask draperies of a warm golden hue were hung at the windows.

Carved into the mantel below George P. A. Healy's portrait of President Lincoln is an inscription from a letter written by John Adams on his second night in the White House: "I Pray Heaven to Bestow the Best of Blessings on THIS HOUSE and on All that shall hereafter Inhabit it. May none but Honest and Wise Men ever rule under this Roof."

THE
FAMILY
DINING
ROOM

In 1803 the present Family Dining Room, located at the northwest corner of the State Floor, served as the "Public Dining Room"—the larger of the two dining rooms originally planned by James Hoban. According to an account by James Fenimore Cooper, President James Monroe also held dinners here.

In the late afternoon, Monroe and his guests gathered in the oval salon—now the Blue Room—before proceeding to the dining room, where the newly purchased French gilt service and vermeil flatware provided an elegant table setting. The guests were seated according to a carefully arranged plan and servants from Monroe's plantations passed the dishes in the formal French manner. When the ladies withdrew after dessert, the gentlemen lingered for a few glasses of wine— Monroe liked to replace the traditional Madeira with a native wine made from scuppernong grapes. Although Americans found the new vermeil service sumptuous, many European dignitaries, expecting more from a chief of state, thought it merely well-suited to a private citizen of some means.

The furnishings in the dining room in President Monroe's time were pieced together by William Lee, a Treasury official and friend of Monroe's, who was his purchasing agent for the refurnishing of the White House following its rebuilding after the fire of 1814. The furniture included two pier tables used by the Madisons in their official residences while the White House was being rebuilt and two sideboards which the Monroes sold to the White House from their personal furnishings. A local craftsman, William Worthington, made a large sideboard for the room, plus a dining table and 16 new chairs. The chairs were all upholstered in glossy black haircloth. Light was provided by four lion's-head sconces, a gilded lamp decorated with swans, and a pair of antique green bronze lamps with stars and swans. There is little information about the color scheme in the dining room during Monroe's Presidency or, in fact, for much of the 19th century until the Victorian period. The rich Victorian splendor was recorded in contemporary photographs and was finally supplanted in 1902 by a classical-revival style.

Part of President Monroe's 1817 purchases for the White House consisted of a large order from the French silversmith J. A. Fauconnier. His work included two silver tureens, one of which is displayed on the dining table, with platters and liners; ladles; a large number of fluted silver plates; serving pieces; and 36 place settings of vermeil flatware. Reproductions of the vermeil flatware, as well as the surviving original pieces, are used for state dinners.

The silver mirrored plateau centerpiece displayed on the dining table in the Family Dining Room is one of three made by New York silversmith John W. Forbes. This one, thought to date from around 1804, and the other two are the only known American silver plateaux, although many such pieces were made in Europe. The edge of the plateau is decorated with eagles. The silver tureen in the middle was made in France for President Monroe in 1817.

A Hepplewhite linen press (above left) is now used for storing silver trays; the coffee urn and tray displayed on the chest are part of the everyday White House silver. A breakfront secretary-bookcase of 1800 (center) displays porcelain from the Benjamin Harrison Administration. An original brass pull (top right) from the Sheraton sideboard commemorates George Washington, whose profile is shown in relief. Pieces from Fauconnier's vermeil flatware, made in 1817, include a vermeil-handled fruit knife, three serving spoons, and a pearl-handled fruit knife.

WHITE HOUSE COLLECTION

Eventually, public functions were held in the present State Dining Room, and the Family Dining Room was kept for the private use of the President's family. By the 1880's the size of this room had been reduced by the creation of a butler's pantry at the west end, eliminating an original fireplace and two windows. The architectural details of the room today date from the 1902 renovation, when the vaulted ceiling and cornice with its classical frieze were installed. In 1961, another dining room was made on the second floor for the family of the President. The Family Dining Room is currently used for official occasions involving a small number of guests.

The painted yellow walls are accented by white woodwork and a white ceiling. The Louis XVI mantel, acquired in 1962, was made in France about 1820. Its decorative relief features a white eagle against dark greenish marble. The gilded clock, made by Dubuc of Paris, is typical of French clocks made for the American trade during the first quarter of the 19th century. It is decorated with an American eagle and a standing figure of George Washington. Hanging above the mantel is an early 19th-century convex mirror with a carved eagle surmounting the gilded wooden frame. Another eagle appears in the plaster decoration above the cornice. The cut-glass chandelier was made in England during the last half of the 18th century.

The furniture in the room is in the styles of the Federal period. The Sheraton-style mahogany dining table, with finely reeded saber legs, was made in Maryland about 1800. The chairs are identical to the New York Sheraton chairs now used in the President's Dining Room on the second floor.

The most important piece of furniture in the room is an early Federal breakfront secretary-bookcase, one of a pair built in Philadelphia about 1800. It is made of mahogany with inlaid satinwood bands and quarter fans. This breakfront and its mate in the Mabel Brady Garvan Collection at Yale University are the only pair of original Federal-period American breakfronts known to exist.

A New England Federal sideboard of the early 1800's stands along the west wall and has a drapery-effect carving on the sliding door of the tambour section. A Hepplewhite-style mahogany linen press—an upright case for storage—has been modified to provide space for silver trays. The linen press, with delicate inlay work, was made in Annapolis about 1790 and once belonged to William Paca, a signer of the Declaration of Independence and later a Governor of Maryland.

The Family Dining Room contains the only equestrian portrait in the White House. Brig. Gen. John Hartwell Cocke of Bremo, Virginia, was painted in 1859 by Edward Troye, a noted American sporting artist. General Cocke, in military uniform, is shown at the time of the War of 1812, mounted on his horse Roebuck. Hanging on the west wall is a portrait of John Quincy Adams by George P. A. Healy; it is one of a series of Presidential portraits commissioned by Congress for the White House in 1857.

Mary Cassatt, an American artist associated
with the French Impressionists, is famous
for her paintings of children. "Mother and
Two Children" was completed about 1908.
The watercolor of a butterfly was painted
by American artist Albert Bierstadt during
a visit to the White House in 1893.

THE
EAST
SITTING
HALL

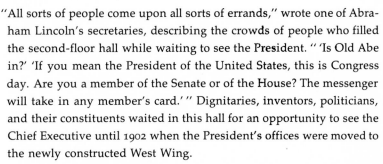

The East Sitting Hall, overlooking the Treasury building, serves as an informal living room for the adjacent Queens' Suite and Lincoln Suite. During most of the 19th century, the east end of the second floor was devoted to official business. When the President's offices were moved to the West Wing in 1902, this area became part of the White House family quarters. It is now used by personal, rather than official, guests of the President's family.

"All sorts of people come upon all sorts of errands," wrote one of Abraham Lincoln's secretaries, describing the crowds of people who filled the second-floor hall while waiting to see the President. " 'Is Old Abe in?' 'If you mean the President of the United States, this is Congress day. Are you a member of the Senate or of the House? The messenger will take in any member's card.' " Dignitaries, inventors, politicians, and their constituents waited in this hall for an opportunity to see the Chief Executive until 1902 when the President's offices were moved to the newly constructed West Wing.

Hoban's original Palladian window with fanlight panes dominates the sitting room, although many of the architectural details date from 1952, including the acanthus-leaf-and-bracket cornice, the outer window frame with 13 stars, and the inner frame with circular medallions. The gold taffeta draperies with off-white under-curtains follow a design originally chosen during the Kennedy Administration. An English cut-glass chandelier from the Georgian period and the pale-gold carpeting are recent additions.

The furniture in the sitting room includes two Adam-style armchairs near the window, a New York sofa of about 1815, a small tilt-top pie-crust table in the Chippendale style, two contemporary easy chairs, and, near the desk, an English Adam-style satinwood chair dating from the late 18th century. The desk and the marble-top chest of drawers are reproductions, commissioned by Mrs. Herbert Hoover, of French pieces belonging to President Monroe. The original desk was used to draft the President's Message to Congress of December 2, 1823, which came to be known as the Monroe Doctrine and which was intended primarily to keep European powers from intervening in Latin American affairs. Some of the Madison family porcelain made by Dagoty of Paris is displayed on top of the desk. The planters near the window are part of the Biddle Vermeil Collection.

A landscape painting of about 1850 by Robert Havell, Jr., entitled "West Point, Near Garrisons" hangs above the chest of drawers. The painting, a view of the Hudson River in the mid-19th century, was acquired in 1972. Although an accomplished landscapist, Havell was best known for his engravings of Audubon's paintings.

Thomas Sully's portrait of the English actress Fanny Kemble, painted in 1834, also hangs in the East Sitting Hall. Sully, whose romantic style became very popular, painted the portrait in Philadelphia while Fanny Kemble was on a tour of the United States. Her nephew, Algernon Sartoris, later married President Grant's only daughter, Nellie, in the White House in 1874.

THE QUEENS' BEDROOM

The Queens' Suite, consisting of a small sitting room and a bedroom—called the Rose Guest Room until the mid-1960's—has formed part of the White House family quarters since the Roosevelt renovation of 1902. Previously, these rooms were used by the President's staff. The bedroom was occupied by President Lincoln's private secretaries, John Hay and John G. Nicolay. The sitting room served as Hay's office and years later as an emergency telegraph room while President Garfield struggled to recover from an assassin's bullet.

During the 20th century, the Queens' Suite, sharing the East Sitting Hall with the Lincoln Suite, has been used by a number of distinguished guests, including Queen Elizabeth of Great Britain (now the Queen Mother); Queen Wilhelmina and Queen Juliana of the Netherlands; Queen Frederika of Greece; Princess Elizabeth of Great Britain, who returned a few years later as Queen Elizabeth II; and most recently by Princess Anne, who visited the White House with her brother Prince Charles in 1970. Both Winston Churchill and V. M. Molotov, Soviet Minister for Foreign Affairs, occupied the Queens' Suite at different times while conferring with President Franklin D. Roosevelt during World War II.

The Queens' Bedroom, which overlooks Lafayette Park to the north of the White House, is comfortably furnished in the styles of the American Federal period. The furniture includes a fine mahogany secretary-bookcase between the windows, labeled in 1797 by John Shaw, noted cabinetmaker of Annapolis, Maryland. The secretary features distinctive open latticework in the broken-arch pediment. The American Chippendale armchair in front of the desk was used by George Washington in Philadelphia. Andrew Jackson is thought to have owned the late American Sheraton four-poster canopy bed which was given to the White House in 1902. Eight New York Hepplewhite armchairs exhibit the characteristic shield back with Prince of Wales plumes and festoon carving. Complementing the rose-and-white color scheme is an Aubusson rug from the mid-19th century, acquired in 1971. The Irish Waterford chandelier was made in the late 18th century.

Above the mantel on the west wall is an early 18th-century English looking glass presented to the White House in 1951 by Princess Elizabeth on behalf of her father, King George VI. The looking glass and the floral painting above it are framed in gilded wood carved in a scroll pattern. Also hanging in the room are portraits of Mrs. Herbert Hoover (to the left of the bed), by Richard M. Brown after a 1932 portrait by Philip de László, and Emily Donelson, Andrew Jackson's niece and hostess, painted by Ralph E. W. Earl in 1830.

The Queens' Bedroom, named for its many royal guests, is traditionally decorated in shades of rose and white. Several portraits of former First Ladies hang in the room, including that of Edith Kermit Carow Roosevelt (right), painted by Theobald Chartran in 1902 with the White House in the background, and Florence Kling Harding (far right), painted by Philip de László in 1921.

THE LINCOLN BEDROOM

Decorated primarily with American Victorian furnishings from 1850-70, the Lincoln Bedroom today is used as a guest room for friends of the President's family. The Victorian period takes its name from Victoria, Queen of England, and lasted from about 1840 until the end of the century. Several distinctive styles flourished during this period, all based on earlier styles and marked by exaggeration of form and ornamentation. The idea of installing bedroom furniture from the Lincoln era in this room—used by Lincoln as an office and Cabinet Room—was conceived by President Truman. The imposing rosewood bed, more than eight feet

long and almost six feet wide, is thought to have been part of a large
quantity of furniture purchased by Mrs. Lincoln in 1861. An 1862 news-
paper account indicates that the bed stood in a second-floor guest room;
although Abraham Lincoln probably never used the bed, several other
Presidents have, including Woodrow Wilson and Theodore Roosevelt.
Mrs. Roosevelt was fond of the marble-top rosewood table in the middle
of the room which was probably designed to match the bed. The ornate
carving on both pieces of furniture, including fanciful birds, grapevines,
and flowers, is typical of the Victorian rococo-revival style.

Between 1830 and 1902 the room now known as the Lincoln Bedroom served Presidents as either an office or as a Cabinet Room. When all second-floor offices were moved to the West Wing during the Roosevelt renovation, this area became part of the private family quarters. The Lincoln Suite, which includes the bedroom and the Lincoln Sitting Room, is now used for personal guests of the President's family and adjoins the East Sitting Hall.

Much of the Victorian decor of the bedroom was placed there during the Truman Administration when the patterned Brussels carpet and the Lincoln bed were installed. The chandelier, acquired in 1972, resembles one depicted in an engraving of the room during Lincoln's term. The sofa and three matching chairs, given to the White House in 1954, are believed to have been used in the mansion during the Lincoln Administration. The pair of slipper chairs, dating from the Lincoln era, are upholstered in antique yellow-and-green Morris velvet. One of the chairs was sold after the President's assassination but was returned to the White House as a gift in 1961.

Near the window is a rocking chair which duplicates Lincoln's chair in the box at Ford's Theatre the night of his assassination. Slender curves embellish the legs of the walnut Victorian table beside it. Round tables, their tops inset with dark marble, flank the bed and are from a set of three originally bought by President Jackson for the East Room; they are attributed to the Philadelphia cabinetmaker Antoine Quervelle.

The walnut bureau with full-length mirror has been used in the White House for over a century, although its exact origins are unknown. In a catalogue of White House furnishings, Mrs. Herbert Hoover noted that a previous resident described the piece affectionately as the "old bureau where I used to do my pompadour every morning." Its serpentine curved drawers and ornamental carving are typical Victorian forms.

Along the west wall are four of Lincoln's Cabinet chairs, believed to have been purchased for the White House during the Polk Administration. To the left of the fireplace is a desk which Lincoln used at the "summer White House," a stone cottage on the grounds of the Soldier's Home—a large Government estate a few miles northeast of the Executive Mansion. The desk was transferred to the White House during the Hoover Administration.

Displayed on the desk is one of five holograph copies of the Gettysburg Address, delivered by President Lincoln on November 19, 1863. The speech dedicated the National Military Park at Gettysburg, Pennsylvania, where Gen. Robert E. Lee's army had been defeated the previous July. This copy, on three sheets of paper, was the second version prepared by Lincoln at the request of historian George Bancroft. The first was returned to Lincoln because it was unsuitable for reproduction by lithography. With it came a request for another, written only on one side of each sheet of paper. Lincoln sent both copies to Col. Alexander Bliss, Bancroft's stepson. The Colonel kept the second copy, since called the "Bliss copy" and now in the White House.

A late Empire marble and ormolu clock, 19 inches high, stands on the mantel in the Lincoln Bedroom. It is similar to other clocks purchased during the Jackson Administration.

WHITE HOUSE COLLECTION

This version is the only one of the five that is signed, dated, and titled by Abraham Lincoln.

To the left of the bed is a 20th-century portrait of Lincoln by Douglas Volk. The portrait of Mary Todd Lincoln to the right of the bed was based on photographs and painted by Katherine Helm, daughter of Mrs. Lincoln's half-sister, Emily Todd Helm. Widow of a Confederate general, Emily Helm visited the White House in 1863 with Katherine. The portrait, given to the White House in 1925 by Mrs. Robert Todd Lincoln, shows a youthful Mary Lincoln dressed in elegant finery.

Used by President Lincoln as his office, this room overlooked the unfinished Washington Monument and the nearby Virginia hills and was one of the few rooms to escape Mrs. Lincoln's extensive redecorating. An observer in 1862 noted that the room "is very neatly papered, but should be better furnished. All the furniture is exceedingly old, and is too ricketty to venerate." C. K. Stellwagen commented when he made a sketch of the room in 1864 that the wallpaper was "dark green with a gold star," the carpet "dark green with buff figure in diamonds," and the upholstery faded. A portrait of Gen. Andrew Jackson which Lincoln greatly admired hung above the mantel. The portrait, attributed to Miner K. Kellogg, hangs in the room today.

Lincoln and his son Tad: a miniature oil by Francis B. Carpenter, a White House guest in 1864.
PRESENTED TO THE WHITE HOUSE COLLECTION, 1963

Throughout the Civil War an inevitable mass of paper work littered the office. Maps tracing the course of the war covered the walls; on the desk and tables were newspapers, stacks and bundles of papers, mail, and requests from office seekers. Two large wicker wastebaskets held the debris.

To the right of the mantel is an engraving of Francis B. Carpenter's 1864 painting "First Reading of the Emancipation Proclamation before Lincoln's Cabinet"; the reading took place in this room on July 22, 1862. The proclamation, intended by Lincoln primarily as a war measure, declared freedom for all slaves in the regions then in rebellion. Lincoln's Secretary of State William Seward advised him that the proclamation should be delayed until after a military victory by Union forces to make it appear not a despairing last resort but an act of national strength.

The Battle of Antietam provided a Union victory and on September 22 a preliminary proclamation was issued, to become effective when signed by the President in 100 days. In this room, following the traditional New Year's reception of January 1, 1863, President Lincoln signed the proclamation—and gave it the force of law.

A painting above the desk, acquired in 1972 and entitled "Watch Meeting—or Waiting for the Hour," depicts slaves and a few friends waiting on December 31, 1862, for midnight to bring their new days of freedom. This painting, by William T. Carlton, was given to President Lincoln and hung in the White House during the last years of his Administration.

THE LINCOLN SITTING ROOM

The Lincoln Sitting Room has been furnished in the late Empire and Victorian fashion to harmonize with the decor of the adjoining Lincoln Bedroom. A small corner room, it served as a busy office for Presidential staff members during most of the 19th century.

The small room at the southeast corner of the second floor was apparently little used in the mansion's early years. As late as 1825, an inventory described it simply as "empty." However, English novelist Charles Dickens, in an account of his visit to the White House during the Tyler Administration, wrote that the room was then used as the President's office, although he was not favorably impressed with either its size or its furnishings. During the Polk Administration, it doubled as a bedroom and office for the President's nephew and private secretary, J. Knox Walker.

The room continued to be used as an office for various Presidential clerks and secretaries until 1902 when all offices were moved to the newly constructed West Wing. It then became part of the White House family quarters. The present decor of the sitting room, which complements the Victorian character of the adjoining Lincoln Bedroom, dates from the Kennedy Administration. The green-and-yellow print fabric on the walls, copied from a 19th-century pattern, is combined with a paisley design in the curtains. Brocade and cut-velvet fabrics for upholstery, such as those now used in the room, were in vogue during the Victorian period.

The four rosewood chairs are probably part of a set purchased by Mrs. Lincoln for the White House. Their serpentine contours, cabriole front legs, and reverse-curve back legs are typical of some types of Victorian furniture. The development of a special laminating process enabled cabinetmakers to bend stylish wood veneers (usually rosewood or mahogany) in imaginative ways. These chairs are thought to date from about 1860. The mahogany French Empire daybed, made about 1815, is ornamented with carved swans' heads. A French seven-light chandelier, dating from about 1830, is made of *tôle*—painted sheet iron—a decorative material frequently used during the French Empire period.

In front of the window is a small desk used by James Hoban, the original architect of the White House. A plaster sculpture group designed about 1860 by American artist John Rogers and entitled "Neighboring Pews" stands in the corner. Genre sculptures of this type, mass-produced and sold inexpensively, were popular in the second half of the 19th century.

In addition to numerous engravings and mementos of Lincoln's time, the sitting room contains early renderings of Pierre Charles L'Enfant's plan for the District of Columbia and 19th-century prints illustrating the growth of the city. French architect L'Enfant was invited by President Washington to design the "Federal District."

THE TREATY ROOM

The Treaty Room—the name chosen during the term of John F. Kennedy to reflect the many important decisions made there—served as the Cabinet Room for ten administrations, beginning with Andrew Johnson's in 1865. When all Presidential staff offices were moved to the West Wing in 1902, it became a sitting room. Since the early 1960's the room has been furnished to resemble the Cabinet Room during President Ulysses S. Grant's term of office. The Victorian furnishings include many pieces bought by Grant for the room as well as others of a similar style that have been used elsewhere in the White House since the late 19th century.

The Treaty Room normally serves as a private meeting room for the President. Since its restoration in 1961, it has also been used for the signing of several important documents. On October 7, 1963, President Kennedy signed the United States instrument of ratification of the Treaty for a Partial Nuclear Test Ban. On September 30, 1972, President Nixon signed the United States instrument of ratification of the Treaty on the Limitation of Anti-ballistic Missile Systems.

The furniture in the room dating from the Grant Administration includes the Cabinet table, several upholstered chairs, a bentwood swivel armchair, a sofa, and the marble-and-malachite clock on the writing table. The Treaty Room also contains a number of other historical White House pieces: an ornate gilded overmantel mirror from the Pierce Administration; a pair of *bronze-doré* standing candelabra given to Andrew Jackson at his inauguration in 1829 by a friend, Gen. Robert E. Patterson; and the small desk between the windows that once belonged to Julia Dent Grant. Two other pieces were originally acquired for the East Room: the round marble-top table in the corner, one of a set of three purchased during the Jackson Administration; and the magnificent chandelier, one of three purchased by Grant. The chandeliers formed a distinctive part of what came to be known as the "steamboat palace" decor introduced into the White House during Grant's Administration; they were removed during the Roosevelt renovation of 1902 along with most of the other Victorian furnishings. The chandeliers were taken to the Capitol, where two of them remain. This one was returned to the White House on loan in 1962.

The deep wine-colored drapes and green flocked-velvet wallpaper

Facsimiles of treaties signed by the United States hang in the Treaty Room—furnished in the Victorian style. The documents represent the ten administrations that used this as a Cabinet Room between 1865 and 1902.

are copies of typical Victorian designs. The geometric border of the wallpaper is identical to that in the room in the Peterson house — across the street from Ford's Theatre — where Abraham Lincoln was taken after he was shot and where he died.

The magnificent walnut table and a set of "walnut French stuffed chairs" were ordered in 1869 from a New York firm by President Grant for his Cabinet Room. During the renovation of 1902 the Cabinet chairs, a Victorian interpretation of Louis XVI furniture, were sold as souvenirs to Theodore Roosevelt's Cabinet members for a token $5 apiece. The massive table, of a typical Victorian design, was made with eight locking drawers so that each Cabinet member could secure his papers between meetings. The table and original chairs appear in an 1899 painting, hanging to the right of the doorway, by Theobald Chartran and entitled "The Signing of the Peace Protocol," which took place in this room on August 12, 1898. The document, which established an armistice in the Spanish-American War, was signed by French Ambassador Jules Cambon on behalf of Spain. A three-handled silver cup, presented to Cambon on this occasion by President William McKinley, was acquired by the White House in 1972 and is now displayed in the room.

The Victorian heart-back chairs, now placed around the table and

THE TREATY ROOM

The marble-and-malachite clock, purchased by President Grant in 1869, includes barometer and calendar dials and a thermometer. Andirons belonging to Zachary Taylor, and believed to have been used in the White House during his Presidency, combine Chinese and rococo motifs. In George P. A. Healy's painting "The Peacemakers," President Lincoln confers with his military advisers Generals Sherman and Grant and Admiral Porter on board the River Queen, *anchored off Fort Monroe at Hampton Roads. The meeting was held on March 28, 1865, to discuss plans on how best to end the Civil War.*

upholstered in black horsehair, were previously used in the Family and State Dining Rooms and are believed to have been in the White House since the Andrew Johnson Administration. Hanging above the desk is a painting, attributed to Francis B. Carpenter, of the reception given for Gen. Ulysses S. Grant in 1864 by President and Mrs. Lincoln in the East Room, just before Grant's appointment as head of the Union armies.

One of a pair of Philadelphia astral lamps from the Victorian period stands on the round table in the corner. Astral lamps were usually ornate and columnar in design with an Argand burner and a ring-shaped oil reservoir that also served as the rest for the glass shade. The lamps were designed so that the reservoir cast no shadow on the table. The side chairs near the window, upholstered in wine-red velvet, have miniature portraits of President Taylor and President Van Buren carved on the crest rails.

To the left of the window hangs a portrait of Zachary Taylor in uniform, painted by Joseph H. Bush. The painting was presented to the White House by Taylor's daughter, Mrs. Betty Taylor Dandridge, sometime before 1890. Two other Presidential portraits hang in the Treaty Room: Ulysses S. Grant, painted by Henry Ulke in 1871, and Andrew Johnson, painted by E. F. Andrews in 1880.

THE
CENTER
HALL

The Center Hall, with its warm yellow-and-white color scheme, serves as a sitting room for the First Family and informal art gallery for Presidential guests, including many foreign dignitaries, who are received on the second floor. The paintings, a number of them on loan from museums and private collections, include the work of some of America's finest artists. To the left of the Yellow Oval Room entrance is an 1843 landscape by American artist Thomas Cole entitled "River in the Catskills." Cole, a founder of the Hudson River School, greatly influenced the work of Jasper Cropsey, whose painting "The Mellow Autumn Time," completed between 1889 and 1897, hangs on the opposite wall. This mountain scene, given to the White House in 1972 by the artist's great-granddaughter, is typical of Cropsey's vivid and colorful interpretations of American autumnal landscapes.

Also hanging in the room are two paintings by Claude Monet, one of the French Impressionists who had a great impact on American art: "The Customs Watch at Varengeville," completed about 1896-97, to the right of the door to the Yellow Oval Room; and, on the other side of the sofa, "Isle aux Orties near Vernon," painted in 1897. The Impressionist influence is clearly seen in two early 20th-century paintings by American artist William J. Glackens: "Carl Schurz Park, New York" and "Clove Pond" which hang on either side of the north doorway.

As long as the eastern end of the second floor was used for Presidential offices, the Center Hall area, originally known as the "Great Passage," contained a partition to keep the public from wandering into the private quarters. President Arthur made the western end of the hall into a "picture gallery, promenade, and smoking room." During World War II, as playwright Robert Sherwood recalled, the long corridor was dark and dismal, cluttered by ships' models, prints, old photographs, and hundreds of books.

During the Truman renovation of 1948-52, the room was unified by the installation of a cornice and book shelves. New furniture and a pair of late 18th-century English chandeliers were also added. The furnishings today, most of them acquired during the Kennedy Administration, include American Federal furniture dating from 1800-1815: the Sheraton settee with two of its four matching chairs; a Maryland sofa opposite it; a Sheraton-style drum table; and two Pembroke tables with drop-leaves. On the Pembroke tables are two black Chinese vases, now made into lamps, from the late 17th-century K'ang Hsi period. The two-part, twelve-fold lacquered Chinese Coromandel screen at the east end of the room dates from the same period and was given to the White House in 1964.

Furnished in the styles of the American Federal period, the Center Hall serves as an informal sitting room for the President's family and as a reception area for the Yellow Oval Room, through the doorway to the right. Vermeil planters from the Biddle Collection flank the entrance.

The mahogany chair-back settee to the left of the wide doorway leading to the East Sitting Hall is one of the finest examples of Philadelphia craftsmanship in the Sheraton style and dates from about 1800-1810.

PRESENTED TO THE WHITE HOUSE COLLECTION, 1962

"Catboats; Newport," painted by Childe Hassam in 1901, hangs on the south wall near the West Sitting Hall. Hassam, a successful illustrator who later devoted himself entirely to painting, lived in Paris early in his career; he became one of the foremost American artists working in the Impressionist style. Like Monet, he was interested in the spontaneous rendering of light and atmosphere by loosely placed strokes of brilliant color. New England boating scenes were among his favorite subjects.

*"Two Girls with Parasols"
was painted by American
artist John Singer Sargent
about 1889. Sargent, who
lived most of his life in
Europe, returned frequently to the United States to
execute murals and nu-
merous portraits of
prominent Americans.*

*"Carl Schurz Park, New
York," looking over the
East River toward Hell
Gate Bridge, was painted
in the early 20th century
by William J. Glackens.
Like many American art-
ists of this period, Glackens studied in Paris and
was influenced by French
Impressionist painters,
particularly Renoir.*

THE METROPOLITAN MUSEUM OF ART, NEW YORK

PRESENTED TO THE WHITE HOUSE COLLECTION, 1968

THE YELLOW OVAL ROOM

The Yellow Oval Room, decorated in the Louis XVI style of late 18th-century France, serves as a formal drawing room for the President's family and as a reception room for foreign chiefs of state and heads of government before state luncheons and dinners. Most of the furnishings were acquired in the early 1960's. New silk draperies and a new rug were added in 1972. Paintings by American artists and two landscapes by the French Impressionist Paul Cézanne hang on the walls. Flanking the west doorway are the President's flag and the flag of the United States.

On New Year's Day, 1801, President John Adams held the first White House reception in this oval room which, although incomplete, contained some handsome furnishings and was greatly admired. During Thomas Jefferson's term, this room was called the "Ladies' Drawing Room," and the President's married daughters, when visiting their father, entertained friends here. In 1809, Dolley Madison had the furniture upholstered in yellow damask and had curtains—with festoons and fringes—made of the same material. All the original furnishings were destroyed in the fire of 1814. After numerous changes in use and appearance, the oval drawing room was furnished in the Louis XVI style during the Kennedy Administration. Yellow was again chosen for the color scheme.

The neoclassical style named for Louis XVI, King of France, was strongly influenced by Greek and Roman furnishings discovered during the excavations at Pompeii and Herculaneum in the late 1750's. Furniture designs were characterized by simple oval and rectilinear forms, and a lightness and delicacy of color and line which disappeared in the French Empire style that followed.

The furniture in the Yellow Oval Room, dating from about 1775 to 1790, exhibits many features typical of the period: straight, tapered chair legs, sometimes fluted; delicately carved chair and sofa frames painted in pale colors; square or oval chair backs; and a square rosette motif carved in the seat rail at the junction of the legs and arms. The round *guéridon* tables of marble and *bronze-doré* that flank the fireplace and the flat-top desks with inlaid wood designs and decorative metal bands are also typical of the Louis XVI style. Brass tips, called *sabots* or little shoes, were commonly placed on the table legs.

The furniture in the Yellow Oval Room includes several fine pieces. The green, barrel-back chair in front of the center writing desk is signed by the Jacob family, celebrated makers of Louis XVI furniture who were generously patronized by Louis XVI's queen, Marie Antoinette. The leather-top desk is signed by the French cabinetmaker Denis-Louis Ancellet.

A portrait of Frances Folsom Cleveland, painted in 1952 by Gregory Stapko after an Anders Zorn life portrait, hangs above the fireplace. President Grover Cleveland, as well as President Benjamin Harrison,

THE YELLOW OVAL ROOM

"The Mosquito Net," by American artist John Singer Sargent, was given to the White House in 1964 in memory of President John F. Kennedy. Dynamic composition and skillful rendering of textures characterize this painting, so prized by the artist that he refused to sell it. Hailed as a masterpiece during his lifetime, it was sold at auction in 1925, the year of his death.

used this room as an office. The white Italian marble mantel was installed here in 1905 during the Theodore Roosevelt Administration when the oval room served as both the library and the sitting room for the Presidential family.

Princess Elizabeth of Great Britain, on an official visit in 1951, presented two gifts to the White House on behalf of her father, King George VI. One was the English looking glass now in the Queens' Bedroom and the other was a pair of candelabra displayed here on the mantel. Intricately crafted from marble, *bronze-doré,* and blue spar stone, the candelabra were made about 1790 in England although they resemble in style the French Louis XVI candelabra between the windows. The "vieux Paris" vases on the mantel, made of gilded porcelain with painted classical figures, date from the French Empire period and were given to the White House in 1972.

Two maritime paintings by Thomas Birch hang to the right of the fireplace. Born in England in 1779, Birch moved to Philadelphia with his father about 1800, and became a well-known painter of landscapes and naval scenes. "View on the Mouth of the Delaware River," painted in 1828, hangs below "Delaware River Scene," a view of the river near Philadelphia around 1840. To the left of the fireplace is a painting by American artist John Singer Sargent entitled "The Mosquito Net," which dates from about 1908.

Above a Louis XVI marble-top commode on the west wall hangs "The Forest," one of eight paintings by Paul Cézanne bequeathed in 1952 to the United States Government "for the adornment of the White House." "House on the Marne" hangs on the other side of the west doorway and the remaining six have been placed in the National

*"House on the Marne,"
by French Impressionist
Paul Cézanne, hangs on
the west wall. Cézanne
used light to define his
subject in terms of lines
and planes; this tech-
nique set him apart
from other Impression-
ists such as Monet and
provided a foundation
for the Cubist movement
which followed.*

Gallery of Art. Other paintings in the Yellow Oval Room include a small oil entitled "Clouds," painted by American artist Albert Bierstadt about 1880, and a landscape, "Shinnicock Hills, Long Island," painted by William M. Chase in 1900.

On either side of the commode are chairs from a set of Louis XVI furniture signed by Jean-Baptiste Lelarge which includes the sofa in front of the window and other similar chairs around the room, all upholstered in yellow cut velvet. The two *bergères,* upholstered in salmon-colored watered silk, are typical of the French closed-side armchairs intended for persons of great importance in court circles. Two *bergères* were included in Monroe's 1817 purchases for the Blue Room.

The Yellow Oval Room was apparently used as a bedroom in 1825 and as a family room during Andrew Jackson's Administration. Mrs. Fillmore found a straw carpet left from President Taylor's occupancy that was described in a contemporary account as "made filthy by tobacco-chewers." She had a used Brussels carpet cleaned, sent for her piano and her daughter's harp, and made this the library when Congress appropriated $5,000 to purchase books for the White House. It remained a library through the 1920's; in 1889, according to an aide to President Benjamin Harrison, the first White House Christmas tree was displayed here.

Presidents Franklin D. Roosevelt and Harry S Truman made this their "oval study," using a desk presented to the White House by Queen Victoria during the Rutherford B. Hayes Administration. It was made from timbers of H.M.S. *Resolute,* a British ship saved by American whalers in the Arctic after it was abandoned during a rescue mission in 1854.

Pieces from Baron de Tuyll's silver service: ivory-handled hot-water
pot, coffeepot, and cream pitcher; a vegetable dish; a wine bucket.

THE PRESIDENT'S DINING ROOM

The wallpaper in the President's Dining Room is a later version of the Zuber 1834 "Scenic America" paper in the Diplomatic Reception Room. American landscapes, based on engravings made in the 1820's by Engelmann, form the background for the somewhat fanciful scenes of the Revolution, including, to the left of the windows, General Washington triumphantly entering Boston in 1776. (The State House, which appears on the city skyline, was not in fact completed until 1798.) Between the windows is an imaginary battle near Virginia's Natural Bridge. The other scenes depict Lafayette and his French soldiers capturing a fortification on "Wechawk Hill," Cornwallis surrendering at Yorktown, and Washington leading his army in a battle near Niagara Falls, although actually this area did not figure prominently in American military history until the War of 1812.

Most of the American Federal furniture in the room was given to the White House in 1961 and 1962, including the Sheraton pedestal dining table and the New York Sheraton chairs, which are like those in the Family Dining Room on the State Floor. A Hepplewhite hunt table with silver drawer pulls stands between the windows.

The most historical piece of furniture is the American mahogany sideboard on the west wall which once belonged to Daniel Webster. The unusual front pull-out desk section is decorated with finely inlaid satinwood stars and an eagle. One of Monroe's oval tureens and pieces from a French silver dessert service stand on the sideboard. This service and a silver dinner service were bought by Andrew Jackson for the White House in 1833 from the Russian Minister Baron de Tuyll and carry the mark of a noted French goldsmith, Martin Biennais. Jackson was sharply criticized at the time for spending more than $4,000 in federal funds for the silver services, although it is now recognized that the money was well spent.

To the right of the entrance to the hall a small mahogany sideboard attributed to the Annapolis cabinetmaker John Shaw displays a portable medicine chest that belonged to James Madison. It was taken from the White House by a British soldier during the fire of 1814 — and was returned in 1939 by one of his descendants.

A plaster composition mantel designed about 1815 by Robert Welford of Philadelphia displays the famous words spoken by Commodore Oliver Perry after the Battle of Lake Erie, during the War of 1812: "We have met the enemy, and they are ours." Also decorating the mantel is a scene from the battle, which was won by the Americans after fierce fighting. Portraits of George Washington and Benjamin Franklin are cast in relief at either end of the mantel.

The President's Dining Room was created in 1961 from a second-floor bedroom as a convenient place for family meals and private entertaining. It is furnished in the styles of the American Federal period of the early 19th century. Blue silk draperies, copied from an early 19th-century design, and a Turkish Hereke rug were chosen for the room to complement the colors in the wallpaper.

THE
WEST
SITTING
HALL

The West Sitting Hall, overlooking the West Wing and the Executive Office Building, was little more than a glorified stair landing until 1902. For half a century thereafter the hall was used as a private sitting area until the architects of the Truman renovation of 1948-52 turned it into a room by enclosing it with solid partitions.

Most of the present furniture dates from the Truman Administration: the contemporary chairs and sofas, the magazine rack and oval-top table flanking the blue sofa, and the Sheraton-style mahogany drum table by the window. The satinwood commode with inlaid flowers and garlands, made in England about 1800, and the English cut-glass chandelier of a slightly earlier date were given to the White House during the Truman Administration. The marble-top table to the right of the window sofa is one of the reproductions of Monroe's French furniture commissioned by Mrs. Hoover in 1933. A pair of late 18th-century Adam armchairs, upholstered in apricot velvet, with painted floral decoration on the legs and lower arms, was presented to the collection in 1955. Between the chairs is a superb Hepplewhite-style secretary-bookcase on which stands a pair of candlesticks from the Biddle Vermeil Collection.

During the 19th century this area was as sparsely furnished as the main hall. Occasionally a detail caught the attention of a visitor or reporter—a special correspondent in the Hayes Administration singled out the "RICH BUT FRIGHTFULLY UGLY CARPET." After 1902, successive Presidential families arranged the room with favorite items of their own to re-create the atmosphere of home. Eleanor Roosevelt closed off the west hall with screens and ordered bright chintz slipcovers for the sofas and chairs; her social secretary considered it "really the most cheery and comfortable spot in the White House." This was where the family gathered for afternoon tea and where Mrs. Roosevelt presided over the traditional morning coffee with family and staff members and guests.

Today's color scheme of blue and gold is accented by the early 19th-century French porcelain vases, now converted to lamp bases, on the satinwood commode. The paintings in the room include works by two American artists, Childe Hassam and Theodore Robinson, both of whom studied in France and were influenced by the Impressionists. Hassam's 1907 painting, "Isle of Shoals," hangs on the south wall opposite Robinson's 1893 painting, "Port Ben, Delaware and Hudson Canal," and another Hassam painting of 1908, "Golden Afternoon— Oregon." The 1855 genre painting by William Ranney, "Boys Crabbing," was acquired in 1972.

Since the original private staircase was removed in 1902, this bright and wide corridor area has been a favorite sitting room for Presidents and their families. American paintings in the Impressionist style decorate the walls.

An outstanding example of early Federal-period furniture made in Baltimore, this mahogany secretary-bookcase is attributed to cabinetmaker Joseph Burgess. Satinwood inlay accents the delicate tracery of the glass doors—with centers of mirrored glass—and scrolls in the pediment. Zebrawood inlay faces the doors and small drawers of the center section. Baltimore craftsmen during the Federal period were well known for their masterly use of marquetry (a veneer of wood and other materials arranged in decorative patterns) and for their fondness of the oval as a design motif.

PRESENTED TO THE WHITE HOUSE COLLECTION, 1961

THE
WEST
WING

Well before the end of the 19th century, it had become clear that the cramped quarters of the second floor of the White House were no longer adequate for the offices of the President and his staff. An additional problem was the lack of privacy for the Presidential family quarters. Finally, in 1902, the West Wing was constructed with a Congressional appropriation of $65,196. The architectural firm of McKim, Mead & White, under considerable pressure from President Theodore Roosevelt to complete the addition rapidly, proposed a modest temporary structure which would complement the mansion; the problem of building "a permanent, adequate, and thoroughly dignified office" was to be settled later.

In fact, the West Wing has remained at its original site although it was doubled in size in 1909 and subsequently enlarged in 1927 and 1934. Additional offices for the Vice President and Executive personnel are located to the west of the White House in the ornate Executive Office Building, begun during Grant's Administration to house the State, War, and Navy Departments.

Remodeling of the West Wing in 1969—including a new driveway and portico on the north side—provided a more formal entrance and reception area for the President's callers. The small foyer leading to the West Wing Reception Room contains an American Chippendale-style looking glass surmounted by a carved and gilded phoenix, a large wall, or gallery, clock made in 1810 by Simon Willard of Roxbury, Massachusetts, and a Western sculpture by Frederic Remington. This bronze, entitled "The Trooper of the Plains," is one of the many pieces of American sculpture displayed throughout the West Wing.

THE WEST WING RECEPTION ROOM: Also called the Appointments Lobby, this room was created in 1969 from the former Press Lobby. Between two sofas copied from an original piece in the Governor's Palace in Williamsburg stands a breakfront bookcase dating from the Theodore Roosevelt Administration which displays official gifts presented to President and Mrs. Nixon. On the west wall is a Hepplewhite-style tall case clock with delicate fan inlays, made for Joseph Gillingham of Philadelphia in 1810.

Paintings in the reception room include a portrait of George Washington with the Battle of Princeton in the background, painted by Charles Peale Polk, and an 1878 copy of a Gilbert Stuart life portrait of John Adams, attributed to Edgar Parker. This copy served as the official portrait of President Adams in the White House until the life portrait by John Trumbull was acquired on loan for the Blue Room in 1972. An 1850 painting by Thomas Birch, "Landing of William Penn,"

The West Wing contains a number of important American landscape paintings. In the West Wing Reception Room (below) Albert Bierstadt's "Merced River, Yosemite Valley," painted in 1866, hangs to the right of a reproduction breakfront bookcase; to the left hangs "Mohawk Valley" by Alexander H. Wyant, also painted in 1866.

"Maine Coast," executed in 1896, is one of Winslow Homer's best
paintings of the rock-strewn shore of this New England state.

hangs to the left of the doorway on the north wall; to the right is Winslow Homer's dramatic "Maine Coast."

The West Wing Reception Room today bears little resemblance to the Press Lobby which was located here from the early 1900's to the late 1960's. During those years, the room was usually filled with reporters and photographers reading or talking in large, worn leather armchairs and sofas—or racing to their telephones when a White House news story broke. Current arrangements give the press space in the area connecting the West Wing and the mansion, where temporary flooring has been laid over the swimming pool.

THE ROOSEVELT ROOM: Morning staff meetings and occasional press conferences take place in the Roosevelt Room. Its former name, the Fish Room, was acquired during Franklin D. Roosevelt's Administration when it contained an aquarium and mementos of the President's fishing trips. Roosevelt's staff, however, nicknamed the room "the morgue" because so many callers sat "cooling off" in it. President Kennedy continued the Fish Room decor, displaying a mounted sailfish on one wall.

The Roosevelt Room, furnished in the Queen Anne and Chippendale styles and warmed by a blazing fire on wintry days, provides a convenient place for meetings of all kinds. A mahogany breakfront bookcase, made for the White House in 1902, stands against the west wall and exhibits official gifts similar to those in the West Wing Reception Room. The carved wooden mantel on the east wall, installed in 1934, displays a bronze bust of Theodore Roosevelt, completed in 1910 by James Earle Fraser and given to the White House in 1971.

Among the paintings in the room is a portrait of President Roosevelt, painted by Philip de László in 1910 and given to the White House in 1971. To the right of the door hangs a gold-framed sketch of Roosevelt's daughter Alice descending a staircase on her father's arm before her marriage in 1906 to Congressman Nicholas Longworth. A bronze plaque with a bas-relief portrait of Franklin D. Roosevelt, completed in 1933 by John De Stefano, hangs beside this sketch.

Other paintings include a small monochrome oil by Frederic Remington entitled " 'Hands Up!' — The Capture of Finnigan," painted as an illustration for a book on the West by Theodore Roosevelt and given to the White House by Roosevelt's descendants. On the south wall is an 1816 painting by the English artist W. J. Huggins depicting the first naval action of the War of 1812 — near New London, Connecticut. It was received as a gift during the Kennedy Administration, along with a small watercolor sketch for the painting which is also displayed in the Roosevelt Room.

Two rare 1801 engravings by T. Cartwright hang on either side of the breakfront bookcase. "Georgetown and Federal City" and "Philadelphia" are part of a series published in London and show one of the earliest known printed uses of the Great Seal of the United States; it was used to embellish the bottom of each engraving.

The Roosevelt Room, a staff meeting room formerly called the Fish Room, was named by President Nixon to honor Theodore Roosevelt who made the West Wing a reality. An equestrian portrait of Theodore Roosevelt by Tade Styka painted in 1910 hangs above the sofa.

THE WEST WING

THE CABINET ROOM: *Its windows facing the Rose Garden, the Cabinet Room was added to the West Wing in 1909. Cabinet meetings regularly include the 11 Department Secretaries plus other officials appointed to Cabinet rank by the President. The room is also used for National Security Council sessions, meetings with Congressional leaders and Presidential advisers, and special award presentations. Furnishings*

include draperies, chandeliers, and chairs copied from late 18th-century
American designs and portraits of former Chief Executives admired
by President Nixon: Dwight D. Eisenhower by Thomas E. Stephens,
Theodore Roosevelt by Philip de László, and Woodrow Wilson by
S. Seymour Thomas. The table was purchased by President Nixon
in 1970 to become a gift to the White House when he leaves office.

THE PRESIDENT'S OVAL OFFICE: The Chief Executive formally meets with all visiting chiefs of state and heads of government in his oval office, built in 1909 and moved in 1934 from the center of the West Wing to its southeast corner. The spacious room contains a handsomely proportioned cornice, triangular pediments above the doors, lunettes above the French windows and above the west-wall niches, and a reproduction of the Presidential seal in low relief set into the ceiling. Furnishings include comfortable contemporary pieces and a number of antiques from the White House Collection. The rug, with the Presidential seal in the center, was specially designed for the room and woven to match the colors in the President's flag.

The office, in which personal mementos of the current Chief Executive are usually displayed, reflects each change of administration more dramatically than any other area of the White House besides the private

quarters. It was in this office that Harry S Truman summed up the nature of Presidential duties with a sign on his desk: "The buck stops here."

The desk chosen by President Nixon for his office was made in 1858 for the Vice Presidential ceremonial room in the U. S. Capitol; it was used there by President Nixon when he served as Vice President. By tradition flags of the five armed services, with streamers commemorating major campaigns, stand to the right of the desk, at the south wall.

The marble mantel, flanked by early 19th-century gilded-wood eagle wall sconces, was installed in the office in 1909. Above the mantel hangs a portrait of George Washington in dress uniform, painted by Charles Willson Peale, father and principal teacher of the Peale family of artists. Executed in 1776 for a "French gentleman," this portrait is thought to be the only replica of another one painted by Peale earlier that year. The background commemorates the siege of Boston, which ended on March 17, 1776, when British troops withdrew from the city; it was General Washington's first victory of the Revolution.

Above a French Empire pier table to the left of the windows hangs a painting entitled "The President's House," believed to date from the mid-19th century. Beyond the tall bow windows lies the Rose Garden, where many important Presidential guests are received.

The decor of the President's Oval Office may vary from one administration to another but the flags standing behind this desk remain in their traditional places: to the President's left, the Presidential flag; to his right, in the position of honor, the flag of the United States of America.

THE ROSE GARDEN: From the west end of the Rose Garden, French doors under a white-pillared colonnade open into the President's Oval Office. The colonnade is similar in style to the adjoining west terrace pavilion which connects the West Wing to the White House Residence. Much as the Jacqueline Kennedy Garden on the east side of the mansion is frequently used by the First Lady to receive her guests, so the Rose Garden serves as a reception area for the President. Visitors traditionally welcomed there include foreign dignitaries and Medal of Honor recipients. The first team of United States astronauts and the 1972 table tennis delegation from the People's Republic of China were also received in the Rose Garden. It is used for occasional press conferences and once, during the Lyndon B. Johnson Administration, the garden served as the setting for an elegant state dinner. The Rose Garden was the scene of the first outdoor White House wedding when Tricia Nixon was married to Edward Cox in June 1971.

Roses were first planted here by Ellen Axson Wilson in 1913. Except for some alterations during the enlargement of the West Wing in 1934 and the renovation of the mansion between 1948 and 1952, no significant changes were made until 1962 when, at the request of Presi-

THE WEST WING

The Rose Garden follows the plan of a traditional 18th-century American garden. Planting beds, with flowering crab apples placed at intervals, form the long lines of the rectangle, framed by hedges of holly osmanthus and boxwood. Springtime brings a profusion of tulips, grape hyacinths, and columbine to the garden. As these fade, roses, anemones, and other summer flowers take their place; autumn flowers — chrysanthemums, heliotrope, and salvia — then provide color until frost.

dent Kennedy, the Rose Garden was redesigned by Mrs. Paul Mellon.

As early as 1800, the first White House garden was being planned for President John Adams. A Washingtonian recorded in a diary on March 20 of that year: "After breakfast we walked . . . to the ground behind the President's House, which [will be] enclosed and laid out for a garden. It is at present in great confusion, having on it old brick kilns, pits to contain Water used by the brick makers. . . ." The writer failed to mention the type of garden planned for this area.

By 1902, forcing beds, greenhouses, and conservatories, constructed in the second half of the 19th century, occupied the site on the grounds selected for the new West Wing. With the demolition of the "glass houses," a large part of the foundations for Thomas Jefferson's 1807 west pavilion were uncovered. This original construction, which had been incorporated into the understructure of a Victorian greenhouse, was strengthened and made a part of the new west pavilion. This restoration and the rebuilding of the east pavilion, which had been pulled down in 1869, clearly underscore the efforts of President Roosevelt and the architects of the West Wing to maintain the original character and plan of the mansion.

F7

*F6

*F9

*F5

*F8

*F3

*F2

F4

G6

G5

*G2

G4

G3

A cutaway view of the White House—
with the South Portico in the foreground—
reveals the mansion's interior. Visitors
who take the public guided tour walk along
the glass-enclosed colonnade to the Ground
Floor Corridor, climb the stairs to the
four state reception rooms and the State
Dining Room on the first floor, then
depart by way of the North Entrance.

Ground Floor
G1   Library
*G2   Ground Floor Corridor
G3   Vermeil Room
G4   China Room
G5   Diplomatic Reception Room
G6   Map Room

First Floor
*F1   East Room
*F2   Green Room
*F3   Blue Room
F4   South Portico
*F5   Red Room
*F6   State Dining Room
F7   Family Dining Room
*F8   Cross Hall
*F9   Entrance Hall

*An asterisk marks rooms
open to the public.

ROBERT W. NICHOLSON

II

THE CHANGING WHITE HOUSE

"Long live George Washington, President of the United States!" A cheering crowd in front of Federal Hall in New York City hailed the man who had just taken an oath of office—blending the ancient salutation to a king and the new title for a new kind of executive.

Thus for decades old forms and new experiments would shape the life of a nation. In 1789 the United States of America began working out a second try at self-government under the new Constitution; and this, for a free people, meant a variety of undertakings: from passing new laws to paving the streets of a capital city, and agreeing on republican manners for a President's dinner party.

By July 12, 1790, President Washington was signing an Act of Congress to fix Philadelphia as temporary capital until the "first Monday in December, 1800," when the Federal Government would take up residence in a district "not exceeding ten miles square . . . on the river Potomac." After long wrangling over a location, Secretary of State Thomas Jefferson and Secretary of the Treasury Alexander Hamilton had bargained their way to a supper-table agreement that Congress would approve.

Ten years may have seemed more than adequate for preparing the Capital. It wasn't. Not until mid-March 1792 did the three Commissioners of the Federal City set up competitions for the design of a building for the Congress and a house for the President, with Jefferson writing an announcement for the newspapers.

George Washington takes the oath of office as first President at Federal Hall in New York City on April 30, 1789. Although he had selected the site for the White House and approved its design, he never lived there.

While the Government remained in New York, the remodeled City Hall provided space for Congress and the first Chief Executive lived in rented houses. A handsome Georgian residence intended for President and Mrs. Washington was unfinished when the move to Philadelphia took place in 1790; once there the President occupied a house owned by Robert Morris.

For the permanent buildings in the "Federal City"—as he modestly called it—Washington wanted "size, form, and elegance" looking "beyond the present day." But for early use, he thought, builders should put up an Executive Mansion suited to the time, and leave anything more to the future when the country would surely be richer, larger, more populous, and more important in the world. When the Dublin-trained builder James Hoban won his $500 prize and commission to erect the President's House, Washington suggested that he omit a third story.

Although Washington generously called the assorted designs submitted a credit to architecture in an infant republic, most of them were more gallant than skilled. Hoban's design (pages 108-109) stood out in competence, originality, and practicality—he included a plan, eventually discarded, for wings to be added when necessary. His unusual "elliptic saloon," today the Blue Room, has drawn admiring comment for generations.

In supervising construction, Hoban met varied and complex frustrations, as did his counterpart Dr. William Thornton, who was struggling to get the Capitol ready. Skilled hands for such enterprises were few; free workmen apparently avoided an area where slave labor kept wages low. Sales of lots in the District of Columbia lagged. Congress economized on appropriations. Materials brought by water came slowly upriver as wind and tide favored the ships.

By June 1800, when 131 Federal employees arrived with their accumulated papers and President John Adams came to visit a city of 501 households, neither the "Congress house" nor the "President's Palace" was complete. Thinking that one man could certainly find lodging somewhere, the harried commissioners had stopped work on the "Palace" the year before to concentrate on the Capitol. Its north wing was available when legislators straggled into town in November, and Adams found shelter if not comfort at the mansion.

His wife, Abigail, during the first weeks of occupancy, penned candid letters to her daughter, listing the problems of a house on such "a grand and superb scale." Not a single bell to summon a servant—officials had scrabbled desperately to procure these, without success. No firewood, in a region of forests—"because people cannot be found to cut and cart it!"—and raw winter weather. Of the six rooms she called "comfortable" and described, none was her own. With some justice she thought New Englanders would have done a better job of finishing things. Meanwhile, she warned, her daughter should keep all these

Time-darkened silver of this Chippendale looking glass reflected the Washingtons while they stayed in the Morris home.

During his term of office, President and Mrs. Washington lived in this Philadelphia house owned by financier Robert Morris. Earlier, when the Government resided in New York, they first occupied a brick house on Cherry Street, then a residence on Broadway. In both cities houses built for the President were completed too late for the Washingtons to use them. John Adams, who also passed much of his term in Philadelphia, prized this graceful coffee urn of Sheffield silver plate.

Mrs. John Adams sat for portraitist Mather Brown in London in 1785. Fifteen years later, Abigail and her husband became the first residents of the White House.

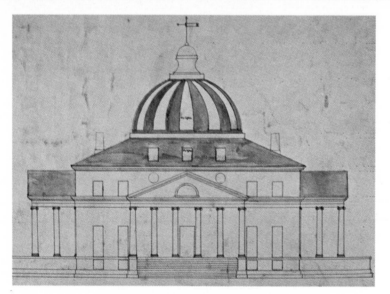

Prize-winning design for the President's House (above) was drawn in 1792 by Irish architect James Hoban. He added an American eagle in the pediment to such traditional features as a hipped roof, balustrade, and arches alternating with triangles above the windows. A cruder effort in the same style appears at lower left, a design submitted by James Diamond of Maryland. "A. Z." entered the sophisticated plan above it, later discovered to be the

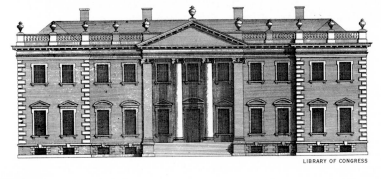

work of Thomas Jeffer-
son. He turned to the
Italian Renaissance
architect Palladio for
inspiration; others
followed such designs as
that at right center from
James Gibbs's 1728 Book
of Architecture, most
popular builder's guide
of the 18th century. Its
idiom survives in Irish
mansions like Leinster
House (upper right) and
at the Château de Ras-
tignac in southwest
France, where an oval
portico resembles the
one Hoban added to the
White House in 1824.

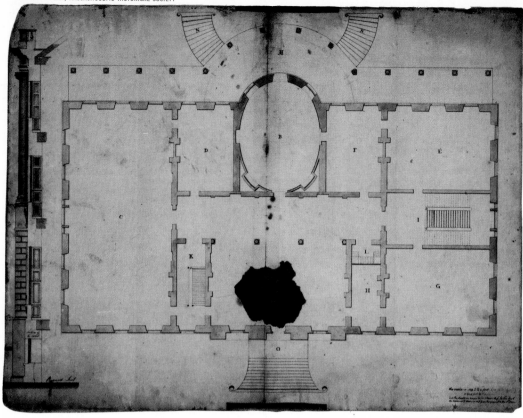

*James Hoban, archi-
tect and builder of the
White House, drew
the plan for the State
Floor (above) in his
bid for the commission.
It includes a portico,
and a colonnade that
was never constructed.*

complaints secret and quote her as saying only that "the situation is beautiful, which is true."

Undoubtedly Mrs. Adams meant the general vicinity, since the grounds of the mansion were a disreputable jumble of old kilns and water-filled pits for brickmaking, stonecutters' shacks, sheds for supplies, rubbish, and mud.

On November 15 the commissioners hired one James Clarke to get the back stairs and a privy built within a fortnight, and then to complete the interior doors and the grand window at the east end of the house. Evidently, when the lady of the White House had laundry hung up to dry in the East Room, it flapped in winter winds.

According to an inventory taken February 26, 1801, the Adamses had a fair amount of furniture at their disposal. The President's bed had white dimity curtains, his "dressing" mirror was "in tolerable order." Solid silver plate included two large "punch urns" with ladles and five dozen teaspoons; 33 pairs of sheets were "generally good," three "Table setts" of china complete. And the stables housed an "Elegant Chariot," a "Good Coachee," a "Market Waggon," and "7 Well looking Horses, chiefly advanced in years."

After four months of shivering in their chilly "castle," offering the most ceremonious hospitality possible under the circumstances, after weeks of uncertainty before the House of Representatives settled an electoral tie between Thomas Jefferson and Aaron Burr for President,

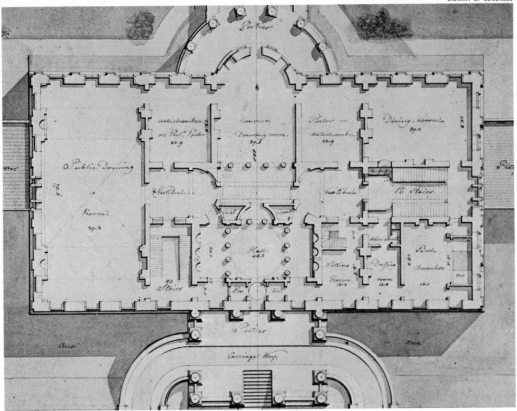

English-born Benjamin Henry Latrobe, a professionally trained architect, submitted the above plan to Jefferson in 1807. It proposed porticoes, pavilions, and modification of rooms on the State Floor.

the first residents of the White House were free to leave Washington.

An unfinished house was unlikely to annoy Jefferson, who had happily spent years remodeling Monticello, but he waited until March 19 before moving from a boardinghouse near the Capitol into his sandstone mansion. Then, as the first President to spend a full term there, he began his efforts to improve it and furnish it in style. The worst of the junk was carted out of the grounds and a post-and-rail fence erected. Instead of finding their way up wooden steps to the oval room that had been serving as a vestibule, guests picked their way up wooden steps to the north entrance. The principal staircase inside the mansion was not completed until the middle of Jefferson's first term.

In 1803, amateur architect Jefferson named professional architect Benjamin Henry Latrobe "Surveyor of the Public Buildings," and soon Latrobe was planning a new roof for the White House—so much rainwater leaked through that the ceiling of the East Room had collapsed. Under the load of ill-fitting slates the front and back walls of the mansion had started to spread. Latrobe substituted sheet iron, sparing the structure an estimated 82 tons, and secured the walls "by strong ties of Iron."

To provide space for household and official work, Jefferson designed low-lying pavilions east and west of the mansion; Latrobe completed these in 1807, building a fireproof vault in the east colonnade for the Treasury. That same year he planned a semicircular portico for the

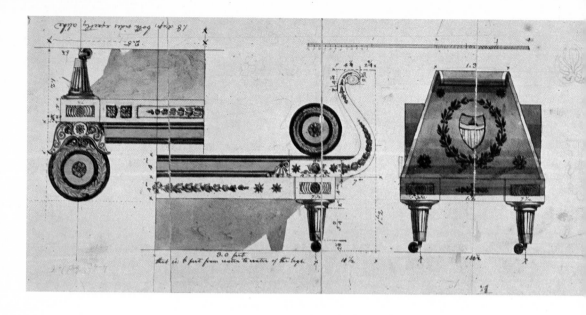

Latrobe, named Surveyor of Public Buildings by Jefferson in 1803, not only made changes on the exterior of the White House but also designed furniture for it. His drawing of the south façade (lower right) included pavilions and terraces completed in 1807. Latrobe's rendering of the east elevation shows the North Portico, finished in 1829, and the South Portico, completed in 1824. Latrobe began his collaboration in 1809 with the new

lady of the mansion, Dolley Madison, to decorate the "Oval Drawing
Room" (today's Blue Room) in the mode of the classic revival. He based
the 36 painted and gilded cane-seat chairs on the klismos—a chair of
Greek design; he adapted the triclinium—a couch used by Romans for
reclining at meals—for two sofas and four window seats (above left).
All were lost when the British burned the mansion on August 24, 1814.

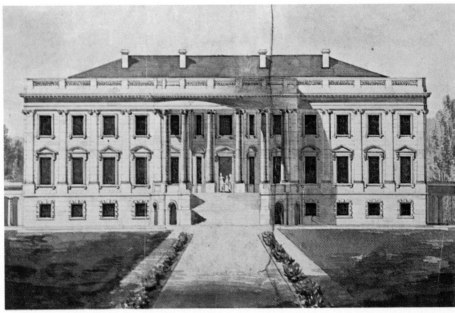

south front of the house and a larger one, with a *porte cochère*—carriage porch—for the north. Jefferson approved these at once, but the first was not finished until 1824, the second five years later; both seem to include elements of Hoban's original design.

Although Jefferson's modifications to the White House progressed slowly, his changes in Presidential etiquette began in March 1801. Washington and Adams had favored a stately formality in the 18th-century mold of public dignity, praised by their admirers as upholding the greatness of America and denounced by their critics as savoring of monarchy. President Jefferson introduced a dramatic informality, acclaimed by his followers as true to the genius of the Republic and scorned by his enemies as cheap in the debased fashion of French radicals. He sometimes came to the door in his slippers; he seated no one by precedence at his dinners—and if this infuriated diplomats, it cost few votes. Between these extremes, subsequent Presidents have adapted the usage of the White House to the changing customs of the country, while the public watched their restoration of a seemly order or their innovations toward a welcome ease.

F or all his democratic manners, Jefferson furnished the White House in sumptuous style. He liked furniture "in the antique taste"—the classical revival manner with the crisp lines and cool restraint represented in France by the style now designated Louis XVI and in America by the term Federal. In his own inventory of 1809, he distinguished mahogany pieces from the "fashionable" ones, with gilding and paint in crimson, green, blue, or black. He ignored precedent by draping many windows not in damask or brocade but in fashionable bright chintz. Unfortunately, it seems that none of his many guests—no artist, no drawing master, no cultivated person—so much as sketched any of his rooms or furnishings.

When that incomparable hostess Dolley Madison undertook to redecorate the mansion, shortly after her husband's inauguration in 1809, she asked Latrobe to design furniture for the "Oval Drawing Room." He drew chairs "to a Grecian Model" with sofas and settees "to match the same," made by John and Hugh Finlay of Baltimore. His drawings survive (pages 112-113), and their muted tints help explain his wail of anguish when he saw the crimson velvet bought for cushions and draperies: "The curtains! Oh the terrible velvet curtains! Their effect will ruin me entirely so brilliant will they be."

In fact the room seemed entirely elegant when the Madisons received callers there on New Year's Day, 1810; contemporary accounts praised it highly. In 1813 young Elbridge Gerry, Jr., son of the Vice President, found it "immense and magnificent"; its curtains—"which cost 4$ a yard"—struck him as "superb."

Barely a year had passed when the British burned the White House. On August 23, while the President was off with an ill-trained army, Mrs. Madison packed a carriage-load of Cabinet papers into trunks;

Fire-darkened and crumbling, the White House stands desolate in 1816, beyond St. John's Church (designed by Latrobe). The Madisons spent the last of his term in rented quarters—first Col. John Tayloe's Octagon House, then a smaller residence nearby.

Relics from the years of ruin: This writing-arm Windsor chair was used by Madison on the night of August 26, 1814, as he sat dispatching messages to his Cabinet from the Quaker town of Brookeville, Maryland. His medicine chest was taken from the mansion by a British soldier; a Canadian descendant returned it in 1939. A tea box from 1811, acquired in 1971, contains wallpaper ascribed by descendants of Latrobe to "the drawing room of the President's House"—possibly the White House.

FRANKLIN D. ROOSEVELT LIBRARY,
HYDE PARK, NEW YORK

PRESENTED TO THE WHITE HOUSE COLLECTION, 1962

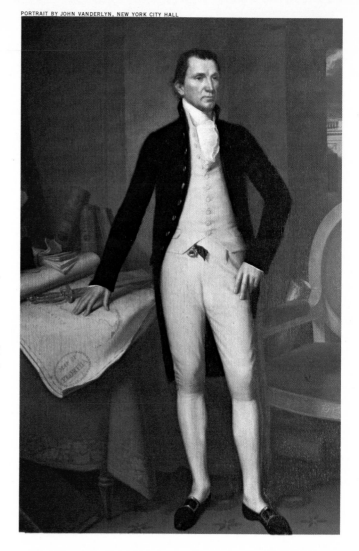

His official home restored, James Monroe stands in the oval drawing room by one of the 38 chairs made for him in 1817 by Pierre-Antoine Bellangé of Paris, cabinetmaker to the rulers of France. Five original square-backed chairs are in the Blue Room today. New blue upholstery keeps a classic laurel wreath and eagle of the old pinkish-red silk. A superb pier table from the same group, also adorned with carved and gilded branches of olive, now stands in the Entrance Hall; it never left the mansion. Baroness Hyde de Neuville, wife of the French Minister, sketched an 1820 view of the White House with its neighboring office buildings (below). From left: Departments of State, Treasury, War, Navy.

Parterre garden in the French style lies before the west pavilion in this English engraving of 1831. Possibly the plantings were carried out by Charles Bezat, listed in an 1822 directory as "gardener to the president."

the next day she continued a letter to her sister, writing "within sound of the cannon! Mr. Madison comes not; may God protect him!" Someone procured a wagon; she ordered the Government's silver put into it. She insisted on taking "the large picture of Gen. Washington. . . . I have ordered the frame to be broken, and the canvas taken out; it is done. . . . When I shall again write to you, or where I shall be tomorrow, I cannot tell!!" That night the flames of the blazing mansion and Capitol raged against the sky until a summer downpour quenched them, leaving the dank smell of burned ruin.

Even after the treaty of peace, Washingtonians feared that Congress might decide to move the Capital to some safer place; and when the decision to remain was clear, rebuilding for the legislature took priority. The Madisons lived for a year in Col. John Tayloe's mansion, Octagon House, then in a smaller house on Pennsylvania Avenue.

Hoban took charge of his crumbling mansion, stripping out fire-damaged stone and brick and rebuilding the exterior walls. By mid-September 1817 the White House was habitable again, and Congress had appropriated $20,000 for furnishings alone. James Monroe had acquired valuable Louis XVI furniture as a diplomat in Paris; he sold this, with china and plate, to the Government — and his agent muddled the transactions so badly that the matter was never fully untangled. To supplement his private collection and some used items of good quality that had been bought for the Madisons, Monroe ordered an array of goods from France for the oval drawing room, a parlor, a card room, and the dining room. He also bought American furniture; William King of Georgetown charged $1,584 in one bill for 24 chairs and 4 sofas.

Filled with patriotic pride and curiosity, a throng arrived on January 1, 1818, to see the President's House in its new splendor. In the oval room where the Chief Magistrate stood, gilded Empire furniture from Bellangé of Paris (pages 46-47, 50, 51) shone in light playing from the hearth and the 50-candle chandelier. Ornaments of porcelain and silver, vermeil and gilded bronze (pages 36, 59) glittered on mantels and tables; on fine silks the sheen was still undimmed.

From that day to this, items from the Monroe restoration have formed the heart of the historic collection of the White House — with the one treasured exception known to have belonged to the mansion since 1800: the Gilbert Stuart portrait of George Washington (page 37) that Dolley Madison rescued from looting or destruction.

One piece of the Bellangé furniture never left the collection — the pier table now in the Entrance Hall. But as recently as 1946, the remainder of the suite and most of Monroe's American pieces seemed beyond retrieving.

Throughout the 19th century, the residents of the White House furnished it in the current style whenever possible. They wanted the fashionable, the up-to-date, the modern, the changing finery of a fast-changing country. They made the best of what they inherited from

French artistry, 1817: one of a pair of fruit baskets wrought in bronze-doré. Bought for the dining room, each arrived with detachable branches to hold six candles.

WHITE HOUSE COLLECTION

former administrations, and thriftily, matter-of-factly, sold it at public auction as it grew outmoded and worn.

Yellowing accounts indicate some of the sums realized this way; but what became of which piece of furniture, at which sale and when, is seldom a matter of record.

Appropriations to keep the White House presentable were routine if not adequate, but a President with substantial opposition in Congress could expect trouble over household issues. Opponents of John Adams kicked up trouble with charges that he bought his seven "Well looking Horses" with money earmarked for furniture. His son John Quincy Adams, elected in 1824 with a minority of the popular vote, met a similar fuss over the private purchase of a billiard table and never did succeed in getting money enough to furnish the East Room.

And White House furnishings take hard wear, if not downright abuse. From one administration to the next, superb velvet curtains, elegant green silks, rich handwoven carpets pass from the freshness of a New Year's Day to the terse judgments of the man taking inventory: "in tolerable order . . . injured . . . more than half worn . . . much worn . . ." to the final "worn out." By March 24, 1825, a clerk reported that Monroe's purchases, "having been seven years or upwards, in use," were "of necessity more or less injured and defaced, notwithstanding the utmost care and attention. . . ." The portion collected for the Madisons in 1814 had become "altogether useless."

Not only changes in usefulness but also changes in equipment for American households—changes in technology and standards of comfort—come to life in White House records. The 1825 survey finds in a private room "one set yellow silk dome bed curtains" for "one elegant mahogany gilt mounted bedstead" with "one husk mattress"—the delicate sibilance of silk is answered in the harsher rustle of cornshucks.

Local artistry, 1817: one of 24 chairs that Monroe bought for the East Room from William King, cabinetmaker of Georgetown.

PRESENTED TO THE WHITE HOUSE COLLECTION, 1962

Much louder but with a similar change of key, the inauguration of Andrew Jackson spoke of a triumph for the frontier and political democracy. "Old Hickory," Hero of New Orleans, commanded the admiration of citizens with no time for polish—or veneer—and persons of gentility feared the mob would reign.

In fact, Jackson took pains to embellish the Executive Mansion. Long-deferred work on the North Portico got under way at once. For the first time a President was in a position to furnish the East Room; it was promptly done. To replace glass chipped and shattered since 1817, a Pittsburgh firm supplied a copious shipment costing $1,451.75 which included 12 dozen "richest cut" tumblers and 18 dozen wineglasses. A French porcelain dinner service of 440 pieces and a dessert set of 412 pieces came to $2,500. After eight years of high-toned entertaining and full-throated politics, General Jackson retired, still a popular hero.

His protégé Martin Van Buren had the bad luck to face not just a

*President Andrew Jackson, portrayed by
Ralph Earl, sits with stiff but formidable
dignity in one of the Bellangé chairs. Like
Jefferson, Jackson lived by a standard of
ease and elegance that never cost him
popular support. At far right, a crowd
arrives to celebrate his first inauguration
in 1829, caricatured as "The President's
Levee, or all Creation going to the White
House." By Jackson's time the mansion's
reception rooms were jammed even on
routine occasions; the local population
was passing 30,000. Below, a view of
Washington from across the Anacostia
River portrays the Capital at mid-century.*

financial panic and the worst depression the country had suffered to date, but the canniest Congressman who ever made fun of White House furbelows. On April 14, 1840, Representative Charles Ogle of Pennsylvania rose in the House to attack the "regal splendor of the Presidential palace." The President was a Democrat, Ogle a Whig. With appropriations acts, bills, and vouchers for evidence, he lambasted details from dwarf walls on the grounds to "ice cream vases" and bracket lights. Deftly he implied that other Presidents' purchases were Van Buren's doing. Ogle made great play with the satin medallion and galloon and gimp at windows in the "Blue Elliptical Saloon." After presenting Van Buren as a sissified spendthrift, he ridiculed him as a skinflint, making the plain farmers, poor laborers, and honest mechanics of America pay for cobweb brushes, churn and milk strainers, and the hemming of 12 dozen dishrags at the "pitiful price" of 50 cents per dozen.

Van Buren had spent less than Jackson. Even a few Whigs pointed out distortions in Ogle's ruthless comedy. Van Buren lost the election.

On a storm tide of hard cider and ballyhoo, William Henry Harrison won the Presidency, began his purchases for the mansion, took the oath of office, fell ill within a month, and died. The first President to die in office, he left his running mate John Tyler to take up the burdens of the executive branch with minimal support in Cabinet and Congress. As the latter refused Tyler's plea for additional funds for the White House, its furnishings rapidly approached dilapidation.

Upholstered only once since 1817, the chairs reached a condition of "perfect explosion at every prominent point that presents contact with the outer garments of the visitors." Those in the East Room, said one journal, would disgrace a house of shame.

I n 1845, the James K. Polks' first year in the mansion, money for furnishings became available again. Victorian fancy took charge— walnut frames, purple plush, rockers in green figured plush for the Red Room, 24 "Gothic" chairs—an early instance of the vogue for revivals that pilfered the styles of various ages in rapid succession.

New amenities appeared: payment of $25 for a "Refregrator" (icebox) was authorized in 1845; gas lights were installed in 1849. Older amenities were maintained. On June 30, 1849, early in President Zachary Taylor's term, someone fitted a carpet in the water closet, charging 50 cents. An attic cistern for rainwater had supplied a water closet in Jefferson's time; running water from a city system dated only from Jackson's.

Although Hoban had added 12 new fireplaces in 1817 and Van Buren had installed a furnace, heating remained a problem. Franklin Pierce had the benefit not only of a bathroom but also of an improved heating plant to make the mansion more comfortable.

Perhaps no President was better suited to preside comfortably at the Executive Mansion than James Buchanan, the dignified bachelor

In a painting full of careful portraits (attributed to Francis B. Carpenter), President and Mrs. Lincoln honor Gen. Ulysses S. Grant shortly before his appointment in March 1864 to head all the Union armies. Costly fabrics chosen by Mary Lincoln to refurbish the mansion suffered amazing damage from visitors who cut or tore souvenirs from draperies, furniture, and even rugs.

who once described himself as "an old public functionary." With the poised help of his niece Harriet Lane, who acted as hostess, he entertained often and genially. In 1857 Congress allotted $5,000 to buy portraits of five former Presidents, plus a routine $20,000 that paid for a new conservatory.

For the Blue Room, where Monroe's furniture had stood since 1817, he ordered a rococo-revival suite that served for decades (pages 126-127); except for the large pier table, the Bellangé pieces disappeared.

With veteran aplomb Buchanan welcomed the first envoys from Japan; in the autumn of 1860 he received Queen Victoria's heir, Prince Edward, traveling for diplomatic reasons under the title of Baron Renfrew. The first royal houseguest made a great impression—for years thereafter people spoke of the "Prince of Wales room." Just which bedroom this was has not been determined.

Probably no President ever faced a crisis for which his abilities were less suited than Buchanan. The sectional dreads and suspicions that had challenged Monroe's tact, Jackson's fire, (Continued on page 128)

Earliest known photograph of the East Room (above), from 1861, shows the King chairs, Jackson's chandeliers—converted to gas—and a carpet from the Buchanan Administration. Grant's redecoration in 1873 (below) resulted in decor hailed at the time as "pure Greek" but later ridiculed as "steamboat Gothic."

Living green meant luxury in the late 1890's. The vogue for potted ferns and flowers,

dating from Grover Cleveland's time, strained the timbers of the White House so severely by William McKinley's term that Army engineers propped up the East Room floor with stout posts before gala evenings. Here, cut velvet as intricate as foliage covers the circular ottoman.

*In the Blue Room of 1867 (above), decorated by President Andrew
Johnson's married daughter Martha Patterson, geometrical forms accent
the contour of Hoban's "elliptic saloon." The gasolier dates from Polk's
Administration, the rococo-revival furniture from Buchanan's. Mrs. Patterson chose the blue paper with relieving panels bordered in black and
gold. On New Year's Day, when the refurbished parlor first went on
show at the traditional public levee, the weather was "most inclement" —
muslin covers protected the velvet carpets. A decade later, during
Cleveland's first term, the room (right) contains Louis C. Tiffany's
decor, introduced by President Arthur. A shield-and-star pattern replaces
the sweeping ovals of the ceiling. A delicate robin's egg tint in hand-
pressed wallpaper was varied with ornament in ivory; in the rosettes
sparkled inlay of opaque or colored glass. From the mantel, below Monroe's vases and Hannibal clock, hangs a new adornment: velvet fringe.*

Taylor's stern obstinacy, and Fillmore's conciliation, neared flash point with the election of Lincoln. When the Abraham Lincolns moved into the White House, a tough group of Kansans joined Senator Jim Lane as "Frontier Guards," to patrol the porticoes with muskets, and drill or sleep in the East Room until loyal troops arrived to defend the Capital.

"A sort of uncanny glamour seems to have been settling upon the city. . . ," wrote one of Lincoln's secretaries; "a strange and shuddering kind of thing, and its central, darkest, most bewildering witchcraft works around this Executive Mansion."

Whatever uncertainties hovered around it, Mary Lincoln meant to hold her own there and make it home. She put warm sheepskin rugs by the beds. Inevitably, visitors were finding the furniture "deplorably shabby." She selected new rosewood furniture, new velvet hassocks, new plush and brocatelle fabrics. She overran an appropriation by $6,700; the responsible official endorsed a wallpaper bill for the state floor *"as selected by Mrs. Lincoln & not by Com. Pub. Bdgs."*

Angrily Lincoln refused to ask for a deficiency appropriation: ". . . it would stink in the nostrils of the American people to have it said that the President of the United States had approved a bill overrunning an appropriation of $20 000 for *flub dubs* for this damned old house, when the soldiers cannot have blankets."

In former decades, foreigners had remarked that plain citizens at the White House controlled themselves with self-respecting good manners. A kind of hysterical vandalism marked the war years. A man was caught "skinning" satin damask from a sofa. Even as Congress was enacting deficiency bills for the mansion, its finery suffered.

Word-of-mouth tradition was keeping up with the mansion's heirlooms, more or less. Lincoln's secretary William O. Stoddard remembered the piece known as "Andrew Jackson's chair," presented to him

Lincoln's office and Cabinet Room as of October 1864: a detailed and invaluable sketch by C. K. Stellwagen. He noted that Lincoln's chair by the window was covered in black haircloth. Littering the Cabinet table are maps, books, and rolls of documents, including long letters endorsing many a plea for military rank or civil office. In a sketch published in 1877, office-seekers crowd the mansion to see newly inaugurated President Rutherford B. Hayes.

by citizens of Mexico. A "unique mahogany frame" and "hollow morocco leather seat" made it "peculiarly comfortable." Legend had it that Jackson leaned back in it on winter evenings before the fireplace in his room, smoking his pipe and resting his stockinged feet on the middle bricks of the fireplace arch. "Mr. Lincoln expressed a wish to have those bricks preserved when the fireplace was reconstructed, but they were somehow mislaid and lost."

As for physical change, Lincoln made only a minor one, long since eliminated: a private passage on the second floor from the library through the reception room to his office. (Today it would run from the Yellow Oval Room through the Treaty Room to the Lincoln Bedroom.) Thus he could reach the private quarters unseen by waiting strangers. A contemporary called it ". . . his only monument in the building . . . it tells a long story of duns and loiterers, contract-hunters and seekers for commissions, garrulous parents on paltry errands, toadies without measure and talkers without conscience."

Nasty eddies of bitterness followed the widowed Mary Lincoln from the mansion: charges that she had taken away public property. Indignantly she itemized things she had packed, gifts from humble Unionists: waxwork, country quilts, homemade chairs. Apparently no one really supervised the White House during the five weeks she lay mourning in her room, and vandals helped themselves. With official approval she had taken a shaving stand her husband had liked, leaving one of equal quality to replace it.

President Andrew Johnson, for all his troubles with Congress, received funds to decorate the house again, and President Ulysses S. Grant carried out a thorough renovation in 1873, at the height of the Gilded Age. Splendor aside, by now the White House was showing its years in ominous fashion. The Commissioner of Public Buildings

reported that a large ceiling had collapsed, "but fortunately when the room was unoccupied." Almost all the ceilings were cracked, and those in the state rooms had settled several inches. The basement he dismissed as "necessarily very damp and unhealthy."

He dwelt on the inconvenience of rigging up bridges from windows (page 138) when large receptions made it necessary to supplement the single entrance at the North Portico.

Closets, he noted, were "now considered indispensable," and the White House had none. (Nobody built closets in the 1790's, but the age of machinery—with its textile factories and sewing machines—had left chests inadequate for the greater quantities of apparel.) Counting the library, only eight rooms were available in the private quarters for family and guests. Everything considered, the commissioner thought "it hardly seems possible to state anything in favor of the house as a residence; but if 'thoroughly repaired,' it would serve its purpose admirably as an executive office."

Of course the White House continued, however clumsily, to serve both purposes at once. If national sentiment was the only factor to assure this, it was more than enough. A President with a small family, like Grover Cleveland, could count himself lucky, but nothing could be expected to shrink the volume of public business.

The callers who sought postal or military commissions from Lincoln were replaced by callers who sought pardons from Andrew Johnson or friendly agreements with Grant, and the paperwork never diminished. Arrangements for Reconstruction in the South and for fast-growing settlements in the West were increasing the number of Government jobs, the scope of patronage, the hopeful ranks of applicants. Lobbyists —even a few soft-spoken women—moved suavely among the throng on the second floor, to speak in the interest of railroads or farmers, veterans or freedmen.

From deadlock in the national life to a note on the Red Room—so crisis dwindles when successfully outlived. Unique among Presidential elections, that of 1876 strained the Constitution to the point of frantic improvising. Democrat Samuel J. Tilden apparently edged ahead of Republican Rutherford B. Hayes in popular votes, with contested electoral votes in Oregon and three southern states. One of those electoral votes could put Tilden in the White House. Behind the scenes, Northerners and Southerners were bargaining. Congress named a special Electoral Commission. As a final complication, the lawful inauguration day—March 4—fell on a Sunday, and tradition deferred the ceremonies to Monday.

On February 20, 1877, Grant assumed the count was virtually settled. He invited the Hayeses to come to the mansion as guests on March 3. "Sinister rumors from W. [Washington] leave us in doubt...," Hayes replied; they planned to stay with friends but would come to dinner— if declared successful. He was, by one vote, but apprehension of some kind of coup d'état or violence still ran high.

Exotica and domestic luxury meet in the Harrisons' Red Room (left), the family parlor: a Tiffany mantel with tortoise-shell tiles; an Austrian fire-screen; Oriental vases and screens; crimson wall-paper with a "Moorish" frieze. In 1882 President Arthur had called on Louis Tiffany of New York to redecorate the mansion in the emerging style of Art Nouveau. The most famous installation was the stained-glass screen in the Cross Hall (below).

American eagle decorates a plate of the
Harrison china, made in Limoges, France.

Grant thought Hayes should take the oath of office in secret on Saturday, just in case. Reluctantly, Hayes agreed.

As guests assembled for a dinner of surpassing brilliance, Grant quietly slipped into the Red Room with Hayes and Chief Justice Morrison R. Waite. The oath administered, they quickly returned.

On Monday, with swirls of rumor about the oath but no violence whatever, the public ceremonies took place with as much decorum as ever. Reporters fell back on the decor of the red parlor for mood or detail. "Its crimson fires fell upon them . . ." cried one; "Red mirrors of a darker red reflected the smouldering light of other mirrors. . . . a dark blood flush, enveloped them. . . . the consecrated and the priest went out together to the sound of merriment . . . the flash of gems in women's ears and the beards of o'erambitious men."

The room is "between the banquet hall and the violet blue Parlor," noted another journalist, and was newly furnished in "the English version of the Queen Anne." The Japanese Minister had presented two small Japanese cabinets. The writer faithfully described the fire screen as "a curious large gilt one with a worsted center piece," but did not mention that Austria was the donor.

Of international gifts, probably none has given longer service than the desk presented to President Hayes, a token of goodwill from Great Britain. In 1854 the crew of H.M.S. *Resolute,* trapped in Arctic ice, had abandoned her; the Yankee whaler *George Henry* in 1855 freed the *Resolute* and brought her to port. The ship was bought, refitted, and given to Queen Victoria by President Pierce on behalf of the American people. Two decades later, the *Resolute* was broken up and Her Majesty had the desk made from the old ship's seasoned oak. Since then many Presidents have used it in their private studies or the Oval Office.

In 1878 Hayes accepted the credentials of the first Chinese minister to the United States, in a private ceremony in the Blue Room. The Imperial diplomats wore their national costume, which always attracted attention at state dinners.

The White House staff — like the diplomatic corps — was growing. In 1881 a *de facto* "Bureau of Appointments," seven persons counting the President's private secretary, had second-floor office space to cope with patronage demands raining down on James A. Garfield. In that same year the shooting of the President by a disappointed office-seeker brought demands for reform and, after his death, some progress.

Chester A. Arthur, whose urbane New York ways earned him the nickname "Elegant Arthur," inherited an Executive Mansion not at all to his taste. One nostalgic visitor had dismissed the furnishings as "modern abominations in upholstery and garish gilding" and the rooms as "staring, pretentious and Frenchy," preferring the quiet dignity of Lincoln's mahogany pieces in their port-wine plush. Arthur swept out innumerable abominations on April 15, 1882 — 24 wagonloads, by report, for the greatest "decayed furnishings" auction in White House annals. A crowd of 5,000 bid high for moth-eaten furniture from

Mrs. Benjamin Harrison, an avid painter of china, helped design the state service during her husband's Administration. She also initiated the tradition of collecting state and family china of previous Presidents. Vast amounts of china were necessary for state dinners like the one below during the Administration of Grover Cleveland. Meals often included 10 to 15 courses.

At the height of fashion: the President's bedroom as Benjamin Harrison knew it. The "Lincoln" bed keeps its original cornice of gilt wood, with crown drapery of lace and fringed curtains. The marble-top center table was purchased with the bed, and the chairs beside the table probably were acquired at the same time. These, from a set of six, stood in a guest room during Andrew Johnson's term; four are in the Lincoln Sitting Room today. Possibly the same order included the chaise, or daybed, veiled by its afghan and dust-ruffles. The massive wardrobe with mirrored doors was probably bought by Buchanan or Lincoln because the house had no closets; the shallow case beside it with flowered curtain provided additional storage. In this and many other pictures, Frances Benjamin Johnston—one of the first women to win fame as a news photographer—compiled a unique record of the White House in the 1890's. Here she caught not only the period's fondness for pattern upon pattern in decor, but also the mansion's typical mixture of the stately and the purely personal: the grandeur of the antique bed, a homely crocheted pillowcase.

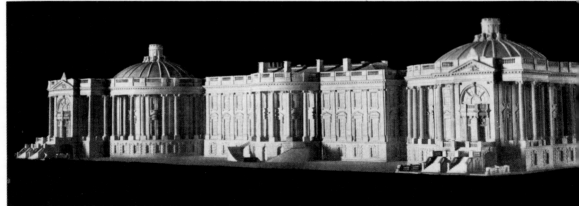

Expansion for an overcrowded house: With Mrs. Benjamin Harrison's encouragement, architect Fred D. Owen produced the first definite plans for enlarging the Executive Mansion. An immense new greenhouse extended across the south grounds in his most extravagant scheme (top). Cleveland's proposal of 1896 also included two large wings, but related them more successfully to the historic house. McKinley's 1900 model presents cupolas—an idea borrowed from the original wings of the Capitol.

the East Room, hair mattresses, marble mantels, curtains, matting, carpets, cuspidors, and Nellie Grant's old globe of the world.

With assorted repairs to make the mansion more sanitary, Arthur called in the famous Louis C. Tiffany of New York to redecorate the state rooms in a manner that foreshadowed Art Nouveau. He found little to do in the East Room but adorn the ceiling with silver and tones of ivory; his famous stained-glass screen (pages 130-131) in the Entrance Hall, now known only by black-and-white photographs, interlaced American eagles and flags "in the Arabian method."

None of Tiffany's major contributions were altered for Mrs. Cleveland in 1886. New lace curtains, fresh paint, touches of regilding, and diligent cleaning prepared the residence for the bride of the only President married in the mansion. In January 1887 she held her first reception and the first of her Saturday afternoon levees to let working women meet the Lady of the White House as women of society were free to do. (Only after 1900 did the term "First Lady" come into use.)

Just how President Benjamin Harrison fitted his family into five bedrooms taxes imagination and record. It included his wife, her 90-year-old father, her sister and then a niece; son Russell, his wife, their daughter; daughter Mary McKee, two infants. Mrs. Harrison soon began a campaign for enlarging the White House.

She ordered green mold caused by faulty plumbing scrubbed off old walls, had layers of rotting floorboards peeled out of ground-floor rooms, and settled down to her hobby of painting china. She decorated White House cracker boxes, flowerpot saucers, and chocolate jugs — the greenhouses provided azaleas and orchids to copy — and her investigations of a decrepit china closet led to the White House Collection that now represents every past Presidential family.

Her interest in history inspired the idea of a "Historical Art Wing" for the enlarged mansion, but that project perished in the wake of a spat over patronage. The mansion was refurbished, with 30-inch-deep panels of blue glass decorated with gold scrollwork at the top of the Blue Room windows. Harrison found the new rooms "much improved," but wrote that the "greatest beauty of all" was in the bathroom "with the white tile and marble and porcelain-lined tub. They would tempt a duck to wash himself every day."

What Americans liked in the late 19th century, generally speaking, probably shows most vividly in the Harrisons' rooms (pages 134-135): the comfort of abundance in figured wallpaper, figured carpets, figured upholstery, tassels and fringe, furniture with curlicues cut by jigsaw, would-be Turkish cushions, a profusion of bric-a-brac. An age enchanted by prosperity found the American furniture made about 1800 —if it considered such relics at all— plain to the point of indecency. Elaboration reached its zenith, and began to recede.

By William McKinley's Administration a return to simpler decor had begun. Panels in the Blue Room evoked the graceful carved woodwork

In the grounds of the White House, the century between 1802 and 1902 saw impressive change — and some make-shift. Just when the first greenhouse appeared is uncertain; the earliest documentary evidence dates from 1857. By 1900, greenhouses (above) to supply the mansion with cut flowers and potted plants had spread west and south of the house. The official in charge, Col. Theodore A. Bingham, fought in vain to save a camellia house in 1902. For most of the 1800's the North Portico

provided the principal door for guests; as early as Tyler's term, reception crowds had to leave via improvised bridges at windows—usually set up outside the East Room. Finally in 1902 a major renovation added an entrance at the east, swept away all the greenhouses, and erected the temporary West Wing of offices above. Its classic lines contrast vividly with the ornament of a Victorian gatehouse probably from the 1870's—and with the plain little house for the guard dog.

of the Louis XVI style. With pale carpeting and walls, white counter-panes on thin-railed brass beds, and white upholstery, the McKinleys' northwest bedroom rivaled in lightness the somber state of Harrison's chamber. From the chandelier, a wire trailed down to the white-ruffled electric lamp on the table below. (The Harrisons were wary of the intricate, patched-together electrical system.) But Victoriana still reigned through most of the State Floor.

Like Cleveland's effort to get the mansion enlarged, McKinley's failed. As the centennial of the Capital drew near, a movement developed with the dream of restoring the city to meet the visions of George Washington and the plans drawn by Pierre Charles L'Enfant. Many agreed with architect Glenn Brown that the White House should also be enlarged and restored to this historic ideal.

Architects of the 1902 renovation and expansion of the White House ordered by Theodore Roosevelt: from left, William R. Mead, Charles F. McKim, and Stanford White.

Thrust into the mansion by Mc-Kinley's assassination in 1901, Theodore Roosevelt dismissed suggestions that the President might live anywhere else, agreed that he should have offices outside the house, and called in the most prominent firm of architects in the country, McKim, Mead & White, known for their work in the historic style called "Colonial." With appropriation in hand as of June 1902, T. R. insisted on an October deadline for the new offices, with more leeway for the state rooms.

They found the Ground Floor in bad condition, and most of the State Floor settling dangerously. On the second story, flooring needed total replacement. Rainwater still drained through the walls in hollowed-out logs; the sanitary system defeated description; obsolete wiring, its insulation worn off, had charred the wooden beams; lack of safe exits made the servants' rooms in the attic potential death-traps. Working at top speed, McKim, Mead & White reconstructed the interior throughout, excavating a new basement for the heating system.

They swept away the conservatories—"Smash the glass houses!" T. R. ordered—restored Jefferson's west pavilion to lead to the new Executive Offices, rebuilt the east pavilion to shelter visitors arriving at a new east entrance. (By chance Glenn Brown—who assisted in the renovation—learned from a New Jersey architect that the east pavilion, generally forgotten by 1900, had been pulled down in 1869.) They provided cloakroom space, an exasperating lack since the days when Jackson's admirers hung their coats on the fence outside.

Charles McKim's painstaking decoration of the State Floor obliterated the proud luxuries of the Victorians. The East Room emerged with

East approaches, before and after: The east gate offered access to the grounds—a shortcut for pedestrians—but no entrance to the mansion suited for large gatherings until 1902. Then a portico that would hold 500 people and a porte cochère, *capable of sheltering three carriages at once, came into service; an arcade in the restored pavilion led to the mansion.*

The enlarged and redecorated State Dining Room of 1902 (above) combined the classical taste of Charles McKim and the individual preferences of Theodore Roosevelt. Wallpaper deeply bordered with floral motifs and festoons gave way to fielded panels of burl oak. Trophy heads gazed blankly over reproductions of Queen Anne chairs. Doubling the seating capacity here put an end to scenes of make-do magnificence in the East Room, adorned at right for a dinner honoring Prince Henry of Prussia before alterations began. A stereopticon slide caught detail, from smilax garlands to cut glass. The makers of this " 'artisque coleur' stereograph," describing the scene, asserted proudly: "It must have seemed to the German prince very much like a dinner in a Christmas tree. . . ."

the aspect it keeps today. Parquet floors gleamed uncarpeted—but T. R. put a polar-bear pelt in the Green Room. Along with Arthur's gaily-tiled floor and Harrison's elaborate frescoes, the Tiffany screen passed into oblivion; the Entrance Hall took on the plain composure of stone. Spare, austere, consciously historic, the White House entered its second century.

Ever since 1902, an authentic look of the early years of the Republic has been the ideal for those decorating the state rooms. Free-wheeling incongruities vanished—such as adornments of the "Corridor" in 1898: delicate blue Venetian glass vases decorated with boars' heads, selected by Mrs. Grant; chairs made of elk antlers, from Arthur's term. When no antiques were available, reproductions served.

Although construction of the West Wing had finally ended the noisy inconveniences of a half-public second floor, the demands of a house for a nation left the private quarters none too large. Ellen Axson Wilson had extra guest rooms provided out of attic space, and in 1927 Hoban's long-deferred third story took shape.

Hoping that the American people would help to furnish the White House, Grace Goodhue Coolidge helped persuade Congress to authorize the acceptance of appropriate antiques as gifts. A group appointed to evaluate such pieces continued to serve, under varying designations, through the Eisenhower years. Before leaving the mansion, Mrs. Coolidge had fitted out the Green Room—and had finished crocheting a spread for the Lincoln bed, consigned to storage by the Tafts, brought out for the Wilsons, and sent off again by the Hardings.

President Herbert Hoover recalled from storage four of Lincoln's Cabinet chairs, and grouped them with other furniture of the Lincoln-Grant era in his second-floor study—later his office after a fire in the West Wing in 1929. Mrs. Hoover catalogued White House furnishings and commissioned copies of furniture used by James Monroe.

To Franklin and Eleanor Roosevelt, wrote one of their guests, "a chair was something to sit down on . . . a table was something to put things on and a wall was something to be covered with . . . pictures of sentimental value." Their own rooms re-created rooms at Hyde Park (though the housekeeper said the rug in Mrs. Roosevelt's room was so historic you caught your heels in it); other upstairs bedrooms had furnishings that might have come from "an old and ultrarespectable summer resort hotel" or "a W. P. A. Arts and Crafts Project." The dingiest items were replaced in 1939, during a general sprucing-up to receive Their Britannic Majesties, George VI and Elizabeth, but the Roosevelts paid minimal attention to interior decorating in the midst of the Great Depression and World War II.

In 1934, rebuilding in the West Wing added underground working space; a new East Wing, hurriedly put up in World War II, supplied three stories of offices and the first White House bomb shelter.

War and cold war did not keep President Harry S Truman from taking a lively interest in the architecture of the mansion, but his controversial balcony (page 148) was hardly finished when the building gave signs of collapsing. The investigation he ordered in February 1948 grew longer as its discoveries grew more alarming; the Trumans moved into Blair House — across Pennsylvania Avenue from the White House — while architects and engineers moved into action.

Between the 1902 steel of the first floor and the 1927 steel of the third, the carrying timbers of 1817 — riddled through the years by heating or ventilating flues, plumbing, and electrical conduits — were splitting

under prolonged strain. "It is a wonderful thing," mused an engineer, "to contemplate the abuses that materials of construction sometimes will undergo before failure."

The architects of 1902 worked under time restrictions, those of 1927 under financial limitations. In 1949, at the President's request, Congress set up a Commission on Renovation of the Executive Mansion free of constraints. Members of the commission sensed a different necessity: to save the house as a symbol dear to Americans.

Various proposals called for demolishing the mansion completely and reproducing it with walls of granite or limestone or marble. But the old sandstone outer walls, with their broad footings and something like their original load, had survived in reasonable condition. Taking them down, as the commission felt and one member said, would be substantial and quite unnecessary desecration.

Private stairway rises from the west end of the Cross Hall to the family quarters. The staircase was removed and the space added to the State Dining Room in 1902.

Out went furniture, chandeliers, mantelpieces from 1817 and 1902, paneling numbered and tagged for re-installation, and ornamental plasterwork — some of the sagging decorative plaster in the East Room weighed 70 pounds per square foot, but the workmen needed a jeweler's touch. Then partitions and floors were dismantled, steel shoring was installed, and the bulldozers began digging.

With concrete underpinning the old walls, a new two-story basement and new foundations, a new steel frame, the Executive Mansion returned to life, its interior restored with fidelity. Only the main stairway changed dramatically, descending now to the Entrance Hall for additional dignity. *(Continued on page 150)*

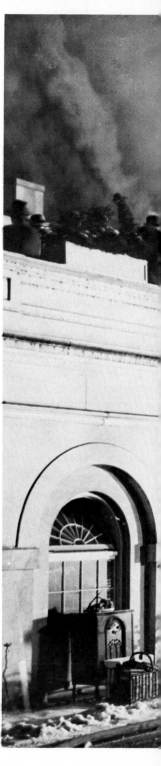

Raising the mansion's roof in 1927 for the construction of a new third story revealed some of the old wooden drainage system for rainwater. Crumbling ends on thick beams bore out an official warning to President Coolidge in 1923 that the roof had decayed to the point of danger. A chute at the South Portico carried down debris as crews working under tarpaulins removed second-floor ceilings, added steel girders, constructed and roofed a story of 18 rooms for storage, servants, and guests.

Fire in the West Wing on Christmas Eve, 1929, brought President Hoover from the dinner table to supervise the removal of papers from the Oval Office. Rescued items stand by a window; Mr. Hoover watches from the roof at left. During reconstruction he worked first in his "Lincoln Study" (the Lincoln Bedroom), then in the State-War-Navy Building (the Executive Office Building) next door. The Truman renovation included fireproofing, supplemented by a modern fire-detection system in 1965.

Jutting awnings broke the lines of the South Portico—if not the full heat of summer—before President Truman added a much-discussed balcony at the second-floor level in 1948. New wooden shades, which rolled up when not in use, did not reappear after the major renovation that soon proved necessary. Trembling chandeliers, cracking plaster, and floors which sagged and swayed prompted a months-long inspection; architects and engineers found the building dangerously weakened. The outer walls stood intact, braced by steel, while the Trumans lived at Blair House and workmen carefully dismantled the interior. After bulldozers had dug a new two-story basement, rebuilding began on new foundations with new load-bearing materials. By October 9, 1951, a crew was laying subflooring in the second-story corridor. After 27 months' work, with historic items painstakingly replaced, the Trumans moved back into the White House on March 27, 1952.

President Truman hoped to furnish the White House with items from its past and with fine antiques. His relations with Congress were often stormy; the budget proved inadequate. He did, however, receive some antiques as gifts.

During Dwight D. Eisenhower's term, the Biddle Vermeil Collection was bequeathed to the White House, and in 1960 the Diplomatic Reception Room was refurnished in the style of the Federal period.

With television, Mr. Truman and later Mrs. John F. Kennedy guided fellow citizens through the White House room by room, and public interest in its decor increased perceptibly.

Early in 1961, Mrs. Kennedy undertook to acquire appropriate items, forming the Fine Arts Committee for the White House. Museum experts

In the third-floor solarium, an enlarged version of Mrs. Coolidge's "sky parlor," a decorating team hangs new chintz draperies and sorts out a new set of casual bamboo furniture on February 14, 1952.

and a curatorial staff assisted its work. A special committee on paintings soon followed. In September, the 87th Congress passed legislation providing that furniture of "historic or artistic interest" might become "inalienable" property of the mansion, with provision for the Smithsonian Institution to hold on loan any object not on display or in use. In the Ground Floor Corridor and the "principal public rooms" of the first floor, it recognized a "museum character" worthy of "primary attention."

By Executive Order, on March 7, 1964, President Lyndon B. Johnson established the Committee for the Preservation of the White House. Its duties include making "recommendations as to the articles of furniture . . . which shall be used or displayed in the public rooms . . . and as to the decor and arrangements best suited to enhance the historic and artistic values of the White House." This order also provided for a permanent curator.

During Richard M. Nixon's first term, efforts to improve the collection met substantial success; acquisitions included 148 pieces of furniture and 46 paintings. Among the paintings are portraits from life of six Presidents and three First Ladies.

Wear and tear on the mansion's appointments—severe enough in the days of Monroe—now reflected the presence of thousands of guests and of one and a half million visitors a year.

Red damask—pierced for sconces—shimmers on parlor walls, fragile caryatids of Carrara marble stand unscarred, and on March 20 skilled hands lift a portrait of Wilson as the Red Room assumes its elegance again.

In January 1969, President and Mrs. Nixon began a major program of redecoration. Within four years it had covered nine rooms: the Vermeil and the China Rooms, the Map Room, the Diplomatic Reception Room, the Entrance Hall and Cross Hall, the Green Room, the Red Room, and most recently the Blue Room.

Today the curator's office not only oversees the preservation of White House treasures but also maintains records of their origin, provenance, and acquisition.

Future generations can expect data more exact than the associations that clustered around Jackson's Mexican chair or the memoirs that happened to mention such furnishings. A list compiled in April 1898, with the help of usher Thomas F. Pendel, illustrates the uncertainties of tradition and the pathos of memory: for the State Dining Room, "Brass pheasant with chicks — Mrs. Grant. . . . Five fruit stands — perhaps Thomas Jefferson. Set of chairs — straight pieces in back — New York City — Arthur. Side board & side table before Lincoln. Plateau — T.J.(?). White marble mantels — there since house was built." The plateau in fact dated from 1817, the mantels from 1819.

D onors throughout the country, who have given articles of museum quality to the White House, can assume with confidence now that care of their gifts has become a public trust.

For generations Americans considering the White House judged it with reference to two distinct norms: a great palace of Europe (whether seen or imagined), and the home of a gentleman (a standard that altered rapidly indeed). These criteria diverged so widely that defining an ideal Executive Mansion was not easy — though of course every citizen and visitor freely passed judgment on the elegant, the common, or the tolerable.

In 1834 a thoughtful, anonymous writer spoke gravely to the point: "This is the only PALACE in the United States. The chief magistrate of the United States has justly a spacious house, while in office, at the charge of the nation, and for the honor of the nation; and yet we cannot but hope, that as little of European parade and display, and especially of luxury or extravagance, will be found there in future, as in years past since our republic was founded."

Now the White House ranks as a norm in its own right. Comparisons still come naturally: The number of private rooms in the historic family section — nine — approximates the number in a suburban home; the ritual of state occasions speaks not for particular but for national dignity — but they crowd less self-consciously to mind.

Suited to its time, as George Washington hoped, in established maturity the White House looks "beyond the present day."

Sumptuous silver tea service and the Franklin D. Roosevelt china set the table for an afternoon party during the Eisenhower Administration. The Red Room reflects extensive changes made during the Truman renovation.

THE
PRESIDENTS

GEORGE WASHINGTON	*April 30, 1789-March 3, 1797*
JOHN ADAMS	*March 4, 1797-March 3, 1801*
THOMAS JEFFERSON	*March 4, 1801-March 3, 1809*
JAMES MADISON	*March 4, 1809-March 3, 1817*
JAMES MONROE	*March 4, 1817-March 3, 1825*
JOHN QUINCY ADAMS	*March 4, 1825-March 3, 1829*
ANDREW JACKSON	*March 4, 1829-March 3, 1837*
MARTIN VAN BUREN	*March 4, 1837-March 3, 1841*
WILLIAM HENRY HARRISON	*March 4, 1841-April 4, 1841*
JOHN TYLER	*April 6, 1841-March 3, 1845*
JAMES K. POLK	*March 4, 1845-March 3, 1849*
ZACHARY TAYLOR	*March 5, 1849-July 9, 1850*
MILLARD FILLMORE	*July 10, 1850-March 3, 1853*
FRANKLIN PIERCE	*March 4, 1853-March 3, 1857*
JAMES BUCHANAN	*March 4, 1857-March 3, 1861*
ABRAHAM LINCOLN	*March 4, 1861-April 15, 1865*
ANDREW JOHNSON	*April 15, 1865-March 3, 1869*
ULYSSES S. GRANT	*March 4, 1869-March 3, 1877*
RUTHERFORD B. HAYES	*March 3, 1877-March 3, 1881*
JAMES A. GARFIELD	*March 4, 1881-September 19, 1881*
CHESTER A. ARTHUR	*September 20, 1881-March 3, 1885*
GROVER CLEVELAND	*March 4, 1885-March 3, 1889*
BENJAMIN HARRISON	*March 4, 1889-March 3, 1893*
GROVER CLEVELAND	*March 4, 1893-March 3, 1897*
WILLIAM MCKINLEY	*March 4, 1897-September 14, 1901*
THEODORE ROOSEVELT	*September 14, 1901-March 3, 1909*
WILLIAM H. TAFT	*March 4, 1909-March 3, 1913*
WOODROW WILSON	*March 4, 1913-March 3, 1921*
WARREN G. HARDING	*March 4, 1921-August 2, 1923*
CALVIN COOLIDGE	*August 3, 1923-March 3, 1929*
HERBERT HOOVER	*March 4, 1929-March 3, 1933*
FRANKLIN D. ROOSEVELT	*March 4, 1933-April 12, 1945*
HARRY S TRUMAN	*April 12, 1945-January 20, 1953*
DWIGHT D. EISENHOWER	*January 20, 1953-January 20, 1961*
JOHN F. KENNEDY	*January 20, 1961-November 22, 1963*
LYNDON B. JOHNSON	*November 22, 1963-January 20, 1969*
RICHARD M. NIXON	*January 20, 1969-*

INDEX

Key references in **boldface;** illustrations in *italics*

Additional References

The reader may wish to consult books on or by individual Presidents and their families for information on the White House during specific administrations, as well as the following books and articles for material related to the White House:

Books: Lonnelle Aikman, *The Living White House;* Joseph Aronson, *The Encyclopedia of Furniture;* Wilhelmus Bogart Bryan, *A History of the National Capital* (2 volumes); Liz Carpenter, *Ruffles and Flourishes;* Commission on the Renovation of the Executive Mansion, *Report . . . , 1952;* Marshall B. Davidson, editor, *The American Heritage History of American Antiques from the Revolution to the Civil War;* Mary Durant, *The American Heritage Guide to Antiques;* Alonzo Fields, *My 21 Years in the White House;* Bess Furman, *White House Profile;* Robert Keith Gray, *Eighteen Acres Under Glass;* Constance McLaughlin Green, *Washington: Village and Capital, 1800-1878* and *Washington: Capital City, 1879-1950;* Helena Hayward, editor, *World Furniture;* Edith Benham Helm, *The Captains and the Kings;* Ona Griffin Jeffries, *In and Out of the White House;* Amy La Follette Jensen, *The White House and its Thirty-five Families;* Joseph Leeming, *The White House in Picture and Story;* Charles F. Montgomery, *American Furniture: The Federal Period in the Henry Francis duPont Winterthur Museum;* Henrietta Nesbitt, *White House Diary;* Esther Singleton, *The Story of the White House* (2 volumes); Margaret Baynard Smith, *The First Forty Years of Washington Society;* U. S. Committee for the Preservation of the White House, *Report . . . , 1964-1969;* U. S. Senate Document Number 197, 57th Congress, 2nd Session, "Restoration of the White House. Message of the President of the United States Transmitting the Report of the Architects"; J. B. West, *Upstairs at the White House.*

Articles: Lonnelle Aikman, "The Living White House," NATIONAL GEOGRAPHIC, November 1966; Hans Huth, "The White House Furniture at the Time of Monroe," *Gazette des Beaux Arts,* January 1946; Marie G. Kimball, "The Original Furnishings of the White House," *Antiques,* June and July 1929; Margaret Brown Klapthor, "A First Lady and a New Frontier, 1800," *Historic Preservation,* volume 15, number 3, 1963, and "Benjamin Latrobe and Dolley Madison Decorate the White House, 1809-1811," *Contributions from the Museum of History and Technology: Paper 49.*

Composition for *The White House: An Historic Guide* by National Geographic's Photo-typographic Division, Carl M. Shrader, Chief; Lawrence F. Ludwig, Assistant Chief. Printed by Judd & Detweiler, Inc., Washington, D. C. Color separations by Color-graphic, Inc., Beltsville, Md.; McCall Printing Company, Charlotte, N.C.; Graphic Color Plate, Inc., Stamford, Conn.; and The Lanman Company, Alexandria, Va.

The President's Park—This drawing is based on an aerial photograph and a plan drawn by the National Park Service. The trees and other landscape features shown in darker green are associated with Presidents and are identified in the key at right.